COMMUNICATION IN RELATIONSHIP

Learn About the Importance of Communication in All Types of Relationships, Get Tips to Enhance Your Communication and Foster Your Relationships to Live a Pleasant Life

Violet Marrow

Table of Contents

Introduction 7

Chapter 1. What Is Communication? 10

1.1 Definition of Communication 10

1.2 Understanding Communication 11

1.3 The Communication Process 12

1.4 Eight Important Components of Communication 13

1.5 Communication Models 18

1.6 Communication Channels 19

1.7 Categories of Communication 19

1.8 Types of Communication That Determine Your Relationships 20

1.9 The Context of Communication 22

Chapter 2. Interpersonal Communication 24

2.1 Interpersonal Communication is Not Optional 24

2.2 Words Do Not Remain Your Slave Once You Speak Out 25

2.3 Endless Complexity 25

2.4 Theories of Interpersonal Relationship 26

2.5 Different Types of Interpersonal Relationships 27

2.6 Role of Employees in Interpersonal Relationship Development 34

2.7 Types of Marital Relationships 35

Chapter 3. Carl Rogers and Happy Relationships 42

3.1 Happy Relationships 43

3.2 How to Win with Your Relationships? 44

3.3 Work Relationships 45

3.4 Essential Elements for Developing a Healthy Relationship 47

3.5 What Isn't Healthy? 50

Chapter 4. Non-Verbal Communication and Relationships 51

4.1 Understanding Nonverbal Communication 52

4.2 Using Non-Verbal Communication 52

4.3 The Importance of Non-verbal Communication 54

4.4 Types of Non-Verbal Communication 55

4.6 Cultural Differences in Nonverbal Communication 56

4.7 Tips for Improving Nonverbal Communication 57

Chapter 5. Dynamics of Relationships 58

5.1 Accepting 58

5.2 Active/Passive 58

5.3 Allosexual 59

5.4 Asexual 59

5.5 Balanced 59

5.6 Close Friends 59

5.7 Casual 60

5.8 Changing or Working Hard 60

5.9 Civil Union 60

5.10 Co-dependent 60

5.11 Cohabitation 61

5.12 Committed 61

5.13 Courtship 61

5.14 Dating 61

5.15 Disconnected 62

5.16 Dominating 62

5.17 Domestic Partnership 62

5.18 Engagement 63

5.19 Friends with Benefits 63

5.20 Long distance 63

5.21 Marriage 63

5.22 Monogamous 63

5.23 Non-Monogamous 64

5.24 Open 64

5.25 Partner 64

5.26 Platonic 64

5.27 Polyamorous 64

5.28 Polygamous 65

5.29 Rebound 65

5.30 Relationship anarchy 65

5.31 Significant other 65

5.32 Sexual partner 65

5.33 Spouse 66

5.34 Temporary or Just for Now 66

5.35 Toxic 66

5.36 The bottom line 66

Chapter 6. Toxic and Abusive Relationships 67

6.1 Toxic Relationships 67

Chapter 7. Healthy Communication in a Relationship 74

7.1 Why Is Communication in Relationships Important? 74

7.2 Over-Communication in Relationships 75

7.3 How to Communicate in a Relationship 75

7.4 Communicating Clearly in a Relationship 84

7.5 Non-Verbal Communication 85

7.6 Listening and Communicating 85

7.7 Improving Communication in a Relationship 86

7.8 Managing Conflicts with Communication 87

7.9 Seeking Help for Communication Issues 87

Chapter 8. Tips to Foster Open and Honest Communication in Relationships 88

8.1 Recognizing Poor Communication 88

8.2 Tips for Better Communication 89

8.3 Communication Mistakes that Should Be Avoided 91

The Importance of Healthy Communication in Relationships 92

8.5 What to Do If Your Communication Does Not Work 93

8.6 Rules of Healthy Communication in Relationships 94

Chapter 9. Marriage, Sex and Intimacy in Marital Relationships 97

9.1 Marriages Need Intimacy to Survive 97

9.2 Sexless Marriages Can Survive 98

9.3 Not All Sexless Marriages Are Successful 98

9.4 When Does a Marriage Without Sex Work? 98

9.5 What Is the Solution? 99

Chapter 10. Interpreting Mixed Signals in Different Relationships 100

10.1 Mixed Signals in a New Relationship 100

10.3 How to Interpret Mixed Signals? 103

10.4 Why Do People Send Mixed Signals? 103

Chapter 11. Fixing Lack of Communication for Saving Relationships 104

11.1 Signs of the Bad Communication in a Relationship 104

11.2 Signs of an Unhealthy Relationship 105

11.3 Effects of Lack of Communication in the Relationship 107

11.4 Fixing Communication Problems in Relationships 107

11.5 Communication Patterns That Hurt Relationships and Solutions 108

Chapter 12. Effective Communication Skills for Healthy Marriages 119

12.1 Give the Partner Full Attention 119

12.2 Do not Interrupt the Partner 119

12.3 Create a Neutral Space 120

12.4 Be Honest with the Spouse 120

12.5 Talk About the Little Things 122

12.6 Use the 24-Hour-Rule 122

Chapter 13. Communication Tips for A Happy Relationship 124

13.1 Simple Tips for Keeping Your Relationship Strong and Healthy 124

13.2 Signs of a Healthy Relationship 131

13.3 The 3 Cs of a Happy Relationship 133

13.4 Relationship Tips and Suggestions 134

Conclusion 137

Introduction

In a relationship, being able to communicate effectively is crucial. Furthermore, it is one of the most important aspects of a healthy relationship but deciphering what your partner is attempting to say can be difficult, especially if they send you mixed signals. Mixed signals in relationships occur when a person expresses interest in someone while also displaying a lack of interest or a desire to keep their distance from them, causing the other person to be confused. We must communicate openly and listen attentively. Most people can improve their communication skills. You must learn to express positive feelings toward your partner. If you're having problems, it's better to act now or instead of waiting for things to get worse. There's almost nothing more beneficial than learning what healthy communication in a relationship looks like if you want to be with your partner for the long haul. Knowing how to communicate with the partner in an honest, transparent and mindful manner is a tool you can use to navigate conflict better and express your feelings—which is critical to making things work in the long run. Communication is the lubricant in a relationship, which is a dynamic entity that is larger than the individuals involved. When communication breaks down, whether it's on purpose, due to a lack of skill, or out of fear of what will happen if we open up, the relationship loses the buoyancy and flow that can be achieved when people are open and clear with one another. Unhealthy communication habits can quickly kill any relationship, irrespective of how much you love the partner, especially if neither you nor your partner wants to change how you communicate. We all want to be connected. We look for it in family and friends, but we often expect the most connection in our intimate relationships. We feel isolated as well as misunderstood if we don't. We let our negative emotions lead to fights—or, even worse, and stop interacting altogether.

To have a happy and healthy relationship, both partners must communicate. It isn't about small talk either. It's nice to inquire about your partner's day, but if you'd like an exceptional relationship, you must delve deeper. It's all about meeting your partner's needs to learn how to communicate in a relationship. You must learn to listen, not talk, to enhance communication in the relationship. A lack of communication can ruin a relationship. Poor communication or the complete lack thereof is a significant issue in many relationships. People in a relationship must be given time to express their emotions; if they aren't, a healthy relationship can quickly deteriorate. One of the most common problems in relationships is a lack of communication, leading to the couple breaking up. People have a strong desire to belong and connect with others. Positive interactions, whether verbal or nonverbal, contribute to your overall happiness. Communication is essential in a relationship to ensure both partners' growth and overall health. Although expressing emotions can be difficult at times, it is necessary for maintaining a positive relationship. Some signs indicate a communication breakdown. When a lack of communication begins to affect your relationship, you will usually be able to tell. Here are some warning signs to keep a close eye on:

- Defensive approach.
- Passive aggression.
- Failure to compromise.
- Remaining aloof to each other's emotions during an argument.
- Inability to connect.
- Unresolved arguments.
- Criticizing each other.
- Receiving or giving less attention.

The lack of communication is usually the result of a more severe issue in the relationship. When these signs appear, it's wise to look for professional help or, if possible, confront your partner. If you find it challenging to communicate effectively, then it can lead to the end of a relationship. A lack of communication will hamper the relationship's growth. Conflict, as well as argumentative behavior, may increase as a result. Individuals may begin doing things on purpose to irritate one another, blaming one another for everything and refusing to follow the rules or requests. In the end, this leads to unresolved conflicts that can't be resolved without improved communication.

Furthermore, a lack of communication can lead to misunderstandings between partners. People in a communication-challenged relationship may find it challenging to understand each other. This leads to misunderstanding and misinterpretation. Loneliness is also a result of poor communication. When people believe they are unable to communicate their feelings to their significant other, they feel isolated. This feeling causes the person to withdraw as well as seek understanding elsewhere. You also begin to see your partner in a negative light. You may start to see all of your partner's flaws. When there is a lack of communication, it is simple to read too much into everything. It may become more difficult to see all the positive aspects of your relationship, which creates a barrier between you and the other person. You lose the ability to set and achieve goals. People in relationships may feel unmotivated as a result of emotional stress. Setting individual as well as relationship goals can be difficult. Without growth, the relationship will suffer, and they will grow apart.

Furthermore, a lack of communication leads to a lack of intimacy and connection. When people don't communicate, they frequently neglect other aspects of their relationships. This may make the partners feel unwanted and unsatisfied. You should work on general communication skills to improve your relationship communication. Consider the body language, be truthful, choose the right time, and do it in person. Once you've mastered these skills, you may need to dig a little deeper to figure out what's causing the issue. You must look for the misalignment of meta-emotions. This is when people's perspectives on feelings may diverge. One person may believe that expressing emotions is necessary for a healthy relationship, while others may believe that it is not. Although couples with meta-emotion mismatches may find it challenging to communicate, it is still important to understand how both of you feel concerning emotions.

From this one, you can plan how to communicate effectively. It may mean that you must compromise and dive into emotions in some conversations while skipping straight to a logical solution and ignoring emotions in others. You must deal with any unresolved issues from the past. A previous event could have harmed the relationship. If this issue has not been resolved, it could be the source of the communication breakdown. Before moving ahead in the relationship, you may need to look back and resolve a current or past issue. It's critical to figure out why your partner or vice versa isn't communicating with you. You should also seek advice from a professional. Suppose you and the partner are unable to fix the dispute between you. In that case, you may wish to seek counseling or seek the advice of a professional to assist you in overcoming the communication barrier. A high level of communication is required in all relationships. This is the only way you'll be able to work on resolving issues in the relationship and strengthening your bond. If you can't decide it between you, don't be afraid to reach out or ask for help. This book explains the factors and reasons for lack of communication between relationships, its effect on your relationship, and ways to fix communication problems.

Chapter 1
What Is Communication?

There have been many theories proposed to explain, predict, and understand the behaviors along with the phenomena that constitute communication. When it comes to business communication, we are often more concerned with ensuring that our communications produce the desired results than the theory. However, understanding what communication is as well as how it works can be beneficial in achieving results. Moreover, communication plays a crucial role in the building of strong and long-term relationships.

1.1 Definition of Communication

Communicate is the root word of "communication" in Latin. It means to share or to make common. We can define communication as a relationship in which participants interact with one another. Communication emphasizes the process of effectively understanding and sharing another's point of view. The communication process is a dynamic activity that is difficult to describe due to its ever-changing nature. Assume you're alone in your kitchen, contemplating. When someone you know (assume, your mother) walks into the kitchen, you exchange a few words. So, what's new? Imagine that another person joins the mother, someone you've never met before, who listens intently to everything you say, almost as if you're giving a speech. So, what's new? Your perspective might shift, and you'll pay more attention to what you say. Your mother's feedback and the stranger's response-who are, in principle, your audience— may induce you to reconsider what you're saying. All of these factors, as well as many others, influence the communication process when we interact. Understanding what the other person is trying to say is another important aspect of communication. Perceiving, interpreting, and relating our perceptions and interpretations to what we already know are all part of understanding. What image comes to mind when a colleague narrates you a story about falling off a bike? Your friend now points out the window, and you notice a motorcycle on the ground. Understanding the meaning of words and the concepts or objects they refer to is crucial to effective communication. Sharing, which refers to doing something with one or more people, is another critical aspect of communication. You and several coworkers may share a joint activity, such as compiling a report, or you may gain jointly from a resource, such as sharing a pizza. When you communicate with others, you share your thoughts, feelings, ideas, and insights. When you bring ideas to consciousness, contemplate how you feel about anything, or find out the solution to your problem and have a classic "Aha!" the moment when something becomes clear, you can also share with yourself. This process is called intrapersonal communication. Finally, communication allows us to convey meaning. The word "bike" refers to both a bicycle and a motorcycle's short name. We can explore the shared sense of a word and understand the message by looking at the context in which it is used and asking questions.

1.2 Understanding Communication

Transferring information from one person, place, or group to another is known as communication. A sender, a message, and a recipient are all part of every communication. This may appear to be a simple concept, and although communication is a very complicated topic. A wide range of factors can influence the message's transmission from sender to recipient. These factors include our emotions, cultural context, communication medium, and even geographic location. The difficulty is why employers worldwide prize good communication skills: accurate, practical, and unambiguous communication is extremely difficult. Communication entails more than just the exchange of data. The term implies that a message must be successfully transmitted or imparted, whether it is ideas, information, or emotions. The sender, the news, as well as the recipient are the three components of communication. The message is 'encoded' by the sender, who uses a combination of words and nonverbal communication to do so. It is sent in some form (for example, through speech or writing), and the recipient must 'decode' it. Of course, there could be multiple recipients, and due to the complexity of communication, each one could get a slightly different message. Two people may interpret the exact words and body language in completely different ways. It's also probable that neither of them could comprehend the message the same way that the sender did. The sender and recipient do not have separate roles in face-to-face communication. The two roles will switch back and forth between two people who are conversing. Both parties communicate with one another, even if it is in very subtle ways like eye contact (or lack thereof) and general body language. The sender and the recipient are more distinguishable in written communication.

1.3 The Communication Process

Mutual understanding is the preferred goal or outcome of any communication process. Interpersonal communication cannot be classified as a phenomenon that takes place. Instead, it must be viewed as a process in which participants consciously or unconsciously negotiate their roles with one another. The sender sends a message or communication to one or more recipients via a communication channel. The sender should encode the message (the information being conveyed) in a communication channel-appropriate format, and the recipient must then decode the message to comprehend its meaning and significance. Miscommunication can happen at any point during the communication process. At each stage of the communication process, effective communication entails minimizing potential misunderstandings and addressing any barriers to communication. An effective communicator knows their audience, selects the most appropriate communication channel, fine-tunes their message for that channel, and effectively encodes the message to avoid misunderstanding by the recipient (s). They'll also ask for feedback from the recipient(s) to make sure the message was received correctly and to correct any misunderstandings or confusion as soon as possible. Receivers can use techniques like Clarification and Reflection to ensure that the message they received was perfectly understood

Encoding Messages

All messages must be encoded so that the selected communication channel can transfer them, and the message could be understood. We all do it daily when converting abstract ideas into spoken or written words. On the other hand, other communication channels necessitate different types of encoding; for example, text written for a report will not work well if broadcast on the radio, and the brief, abbreviated text used during text messages would be inappropriate in a letter or speech. A graph, chart, or other visualization may be the best way to communicate complex data. Good communicators encode the messages to fit the channel as well as the target audience. They use accurate language to convey information clearly and concisely. They also foresee and eliminate potential sources of ambiguity and misunderstanding. They are fully aware of the recipients' previous experience decoding similar messages. Encoding messages correctly for the intended audience and channel is a crucial skill in communicating effectively.

Decoding Messages

The recipient must decode the message once it has been received. Decoding is also an important communication skill. Messages would be decoded and understood in a variety of ways. This will be determined by their prior experience and understanding of the message's context, their familiarity with the sender, the psychological state, how they feel, communication barriers, and the time and place of receipt. As a result, a variety of factors will influence decoding and comprehension. Successful communicators are aware of how the message will be decoded and anticipate and eliminate as many possible causes of misunderstanding as possible.

Feedback

Feedback is the last part of communication: the recipient informs the sender that he has received and comprehended the message. Message recipients are likely to express their understanding of the messages both through verbal and nonverbal reactions. Effective communicators pay special attention to this feedback because it is the only way to determine whether the message was received correctly and correct any misunderstandings. Keep in mind that the amount and type of feedback you receive will vary depending on the communication channel. Feedback given during a telephone or face-to-face conversation is immediate and direct, whereas feedback provided in response to messages broadcast on television or radio is indirect and may be delayed or even given through other media such as the Internet.

1.4 Eight Important Components of Communication

It would be easy to understand the communication process if

we can segment it into eight essential components. These essential components are listed below:

- Source

- Message
- Channel
- Receiver
- Feedback
- Environment
- Context
- Interference

Each of these eight elements plays an essential role in the overall process. These elements will now be explained.

Source

The message is imagined, created, and sent by the source. The source in a public speaking situation is the person who is giving the speech. He or she communicates the message to the audience by providing new information. The speaker also sends a message with his or her voice tone, body language, and clothing choices. The speaker starts by deciding on the message: what to say and how to say it. The second step entails encoding the message by selecting the perfect order or words to convey the desired meaning. The information is then presented or sent to the audience or receiver in the third step. Finally, the source determines how well the message was received by watching the audience's reaction and responds appropriately with clarification or additional information.

Message

The response or meaning generated by the source for the audience or receiver is known as the message. When giving a speech or writing a report, the message may appear to be nothing more than the words you select to convey the meaning. But that is only the start. Grammar and organization are used to bring the words together. You might want to put the most important point last. The way you say it—in a speech, with your voice's tone, body language, and appearance—and in a report, with the writing style, punctuation, as well as the headings and formatting you choose—all contribute to the message.

Furthermore, part of the message could be the environment or context in which it is delivered, as well as the noise that may make your message difficult to hear or see. Consider the following scenario: you're speaking to a large group of salespeople, and you're aware that the World Series will be played tonight. You could start by saying, "I fully comprehend there is an important game tonight." If your audience has trouble settling down, you could say, "I realize there is an important game tonight." By verbally expressing something that most of your audience is aware of and interested in, you can capture and focus their attention.

Channel

The channel is the path taken by a message or messages between the sender and the receiver. Consider your television, for example. On your television, there must be several channels that you watch. Even in a digital world, each channel takes up some space in the cable or signal that delivers the message of every other channel to your home. The audio signal you hear is

combined with the visual movement you see on television. They send the message to the audience or receiver as a group. Turn down the television's volume. Can you still make sense of what's going on? You can do this a lot of the time because the show's body language conveys a lot of the message. Turn around so you can't see the television while turning up the volume. The dialogue is still audible, and the plot is still clear.

Similarly, you use a channel to communicate your message when you speak or write. Telephone conversations, speeches, face-to-face conversations, voice mail messages, radio, public address systems, and voice over Internet protocol are examples of spoken channels (VoIP). Purchase orders, letters, invoices, memorandums, blogs, e-mail, text messages, tweets, newspaper and magazine articles and other channels are examples of written media.

Receiver

The receiver receives the message from the source, and he analyzes and interprets it in ways that the source intended and unintended. Consider a football receiver to gain a better understanding of this component. The quarterback tosses the ball (message) to a receiver, who should see and interpret where the ball will be caught. The quarterback could intend for the receiver to "catch" his message in one way, but the receiver may interpret things differently and completely miss the football (and its intended meaning). To receive a message, you see, listen, touch, smell, and taste. Long before you come on stage and open your mouth, your audience assesses you in the same way that you evaluate them. The nonverbal responses of the audience can provide insight into how you should adjust your opening. You can predict what you would look for if you were in their shoes by imagining yourself in their shoes. You can understand the interaction between receiver and source in a business communication context just like a quarterback prepares where the receiver would be to place the ball correctly. All of this occurs simultaneously, demonstrating why and how communication is constantly evolving.

Feedback

You are providing feedback when you respond to the source, whether intentionally or unintentionally. The messages that the receiver sends back to the source are known as feedback. All of these feedback signals, whether verbal or nonverbal, allow the authority to determine how well and accurately and poorly and inaccurately the message was received. The receiver or audience can also use feedback to ask for clarification, agree or disagree, or suggest ways for the source to make the message quite interesting. As the amount of feedback grows, so does the accuracy of communication. Assume you're a sales manager, and you're on a conference call with four other salespeople. As the source, you'd like to advise the reps to take advantage of the fact that it's World Series season to close sales on baseball-related sporting goods. You deliver your message, but there are no responses from your audience. You could perhaps assume that this implies they identified and agreed with you, but you might be disappointed later in the month to discover that very few sales were generated. If you followed up with a request for feedback, you might be able to clarify your message and learn whether any of the sales representatives thought your suggestion would be ineffective with their customers.

Environment

The physical and psychological environment in which you send and receive messages is referred to as the environment. The room's chairs, tables, lighting, and sound equipment can all be considered part of the environment. The room exemplifies the environment. The setting can also include formal attire, which can indicate whether a conversation is open and caring or more formal and professional. When people are physically close to each other, they are more likely to have an intimate conversation than when they could only see each other from across the room. They could text each other in that case, which is a private form of communication. The environment has an impact on the decision to text. Your surroundings will influence and play a major role in your speech as a speaker. It's always a great idea to check out the venue where you'll be speaking before the big day.

Context

The scene, setting and expectations of the individuals involved all contribute to the context of the communication interaction. Business suits (environmental cues) may be evident in a professional communication context, influencing participants' language and behavior expectations directly or indirectly. A presentation or a discussion is not a one-time occurrence. You came from somewhere when you came to class. The person next to you, as well as the instructor, felt the same way. The participants' contextual communication expectations determine the extent to which the environment is formal and informal. The said instructor may be used to verbal and nonverbal exhibits of respect in the academic environment, whereas the man sitting next to you could be used for informal communication with instructors. You may be accustomed to

formal interactions with instructors and regard your classmate's question, "Hey Teacher, do we have homework today?" as rude and inconsiderate when you consider it to be expected. The instructor's nonverbal response will almost certainly reveal how they perceive the interaction, both in terms of word choice and delivery. Context refers to what people expect from one another, and we frequently form those expectations based on external cues. Traditional gatherings, such as weddings or birthday parties, are often formal affairs. There is a moment for quiet social greetings, a moment for silence as the bride walks down the aisle, and a time for the father to dance with his daughter as she transitions from a girl to a woman in the eyes of her community. There may be a time for a raucous celebration and dancing in either celebration. You might be asked to make a toast. The wedding or other context will influence the presentation, timing, and usefulness. Who speaks first in a business meeting? This is most likely related to each person's position and role outside of the meeting. Context is extremely important in communication, especially when communicating across cultures.

Interference

Interference, also known as noise, can come from a variety of places. Interference is defined as anything that prevents or alters the message's intended meaning as determined by the source. For example, if you drove to work or school in a car, you were almost certainly surrounded by noise. Billboards, car horns or the radio in your vehicle may have interrupted your thoughts or a conversation with a fellow passenger. When your thoughts take over your attention while listening to or reading a message, this is referred to as psychological noise. Imagine it is 4:45 p.m., and your boss, who is in another city for a meeting, sends you an e-mail asking for last month's revenue figures, an

analysis of the current sales projections, and sales figures from the same month in the previous five years. You may open the e-mail and begin reading, talking to yourself, "Great—no problem—I have the figures and also that analysis right here on my computer." You send a response that includes the previous month's sales figures as well as current projections. After that, at 5 p.m., you turn off the computer and then go home. The next morning, your boss calls to tell you that he was inconvenienced because you failed to include previous year's sales figures. What exactly was the issue? Interference: by imagining how you wanted to respond to your boss's message, you stopped yourself from reading the entire message attentively.

Interference can also come from other places. Maybe you're hungry, and your focus on the present moment is interfering with the ability to listen. Perhaps the office is stuffy and hot. How might this affect your ability to attend and participate if you were a member of an audience listening to an executive speech? The normal encoding and decoding of the message carried by the channel between the source and the receiver are disrupted by noise. Although not all noise is harmful, it does obstruct communication. Your cell phone ringtone, for example, maybe a pleasant sound to you, but it may disrupt class communication and annoy your classmates.

1.5 Communication Models

Researchers have discovered that when two people communicate, the source and receiver may send messages simultaneously, with messages frequently overlapping. As the speaker, you will often take on the roles of both source and receiver. You'll concentrate on the delivery and reception of your messages to the audience. The audience will react in the form of feedback, which will provide you with crucial

information. While there are many communication models to choose from, there are two specific channels that provide perspectives and lessons for business communicators. Researchers frequently view communication as a transactional process, with actions often occurring simultaneously, rather than viewing the source sending a message and the recipient receiving it as two separate acts. In conversational turn-taking, for instance, the differentiation between the source and the receiver is blurred because both participants play both roles simultaneously.

1.6 Communication Channels

It is the term used to describe how we communicate. As a result, it is how we send a message to a recipient or receive a message from someone else. Today, we have access to a variety of communication channels. Face-to-face conversations, text messages, phone calls, email, and the Internet, including social media sites like Facebook and Twitter, radio and television, written letters, brochures, and reports, are examples. Effective communication necessitates the selection of an appropriate communication channel. Each communication channel has its own set of advantages and disadvantages. For example, sending a written letter to one or two people with news of an upcoming event may effectively communicate the message. However, it will not be a time- or cost-effective method of reaching many people.

On the other hand, a printed document effectively conveys complex technical information than a spoken message. The recipients can take their time digesting the information and go over anything they don't fully comprehend. Written communication can also be used to keep track of what has been said, for example, when taking minutes at a meeting.

1.7 Categories of Communication

We communicate in various ways, and more than one may be active at any given time. The following are the various categories of communication:

Spoken or Verbal Communication

It includes telephone, face-to-face, radio or television as well as other media.

Non-Verbal Communication

Gestures, body language, the way we act or dress, where we stand, and sometimes even our scent are all the factors that come in the domain of non-verbal communication. We communicate with others in a variety of subtle ways (perhaps even unintentionally). The tone of one's voice, for example, can reveal one's mood and emotional state, while hand signals and gestures can complement a spoken message.

Written Communication

E-mails, letters, social media, magazines, books, the Internet, and other forms of media are all included in this category. Until recently, when it came to communicating the written word, a comparatively small number of writers and publishers wielded enormous power. We can all write as well as publish our thoughts on the Internet. This has resulted in a proliferation of communication and information options.

Visualizations

It includes maps, charts, graphs and logos, and other visualizations. All of these can communicate messages.

1.8 Types of Communication That Determine Your Relationships

To begin and maintain a relationship, various types of communication are required. Optical, auditory, emotional, nonverbal, and verbal are the five types of communication. Sending and receiving messages is the most basic form of communication. Messages are disseminated in a variety of ways. You will be a master at forming and maintaining strong personal and professional relationships once you understand and apply all types of communication.

Optical

Optical communication entails seeing someone, keeping your gaze fixed on them, and noticing their presence. Optical communication begins when your peepers notice another

person, as well as their peepers, notice you. You notice their appearance, clothing, hairdo, facial expression, body position, and body type and immediately think to yourself, "I like what I see," or "I'll look elsewhere." If you like what you see as well as the other person likes what they see, you'll have to make a new decision about "the next step." You or the other person will figure out how to get closer and start the second kind of effective communication.

Auditory

The most important type of communication is auditory communication. Listening to communication is what it's all about. Have you ever said something like "my dog just died" and had someone respond with "that's nice"?

Why would someone say that your dog's death was a good thing? Because they weren't paying attention, weren't tuned in, and weren't interested. What was your reaction to that? Do you assume you would have received a better response if the person had been "tuned in" and listened to what you had to say if they had been "tuned in" and listened to what you had to say? The response would have been far more appropriate, emphasizing the importance of listening. There is a greater probability of you taking upon another type of communication, emotional communication when you are tuned in and listening to the other person.

Emotional

Emotional communication is critical to all aspects of starting and progressing in a relationship, to the point where Facebook finally added five new reaction emoji to its "Like" button. These buttons enable people to react to a post with more than just alike. They can now express emotions such as laughter, love,

anger, sadness, and astonishment. What is the significance of Facebook making this change to their Like button? People can react more emotionally and appropriately to messages when they use these five emoji. You'll now get the "sad emoji" instead of "likes" when you post that your dog died, letting you know that others are concerned. Can you see how crucial emotional communication is in a relationship? Whether in a professional or personal relationship, an appropriate response is more likely to keep the relationship moving forward.

Non-Verbal

Pauses, tone of voice, speech rate, facial expressions, and body positions are all examples of nonverbal communication (i.e., crossed arms). Nonverbal communication includes even walking away. If someone smiles at you while talking to them, you'll likely feel validated and that things are going well. When someone frowns in response to something you say, you know that they don't agree with you. Nonverbal cues impact how people in a relationship understand each other's spoken and unspoken communication.

Verbal

Language is used in the form of sentences, phrases, as well as dialogue in verbal communication. It's much more than that in reality. Spoken words can be misunderstood. However, there is a way to avoid having your words misunderstood. Speak up and keep an eye out for signs of acceptance. If you pay close attention, you'll notice that you can use words in the sentences, phrases, and dialogues that resonate more strongly with the other person, resulting in a positive communication experience. More positive experiences will result from a positive communication experience. This implies more enjoyable

interactions, which will help to maintain and advance the relationship. By now, you've developed a more holistic approach to relationship communication. Here's a hint: use expressions when speaking to the other person and look for clues in how the other person listens, looks, and reacts to you.

1.9 The Context of Communication

Every piece of communication has a context. This implies that communication takes place for a specific reason. One or more of the participants may overlook the context, causing communication to fail. Everyone must understand the context of the communication to avoid misunderstandings and thus communicate more effectively. What is the purpose of communication? Participants must be on the same 'wavelength' to understand why the communication is taking place. Explaining why something is happening could be a good way to start a larger conversation. Knowing why contact occurs is an essential step; however, some issues affect the communication's context:

Timing

The importance of timing ineffective communication cannot be overstated. Along with deciding on a good time to have a conversation, make sure there is enough time to cover everything that needs to be protected, including time to clarify and negotiate. Speaking with an employee regarding a tactical decision five minutes before they have to leave the office for the day, for instance, is unlikely to yield the same results as having the same conversation the next morning.

Location

It should be self-evident that communication will be less effective if it occurs in a noisy, uncomfortable, or crowded environment. There are numerous distractions in such places, as well as a lack of privacy.

Misconceptions

Our feelings about communication influence the context of communication. As previously stated, we stereotype people, which can lead to incorrect assumptions and misconceptions. When communicating, we may assume that:

- All parties are aware of what we are discussing.
- We are aware of the other person's perspectives and opinions on the situation.
- We should not show emotion.
- We are correct, and they are incorrect.

Chapter 2
Interpersonal Communication

The association, connection, interaction, and bond between two or more people are interpersonal relationships. Some basic principles apply to all interpersonal communications. The effectiveness of your communications is governed by these principles, which are simple to understand but challenging to master. We will now explain these concepts and provides examples of how, why, and when interpersonal communication takes place.

2.1 Interpersonal Communication is Not Optional

We may try to avoid communicating at times, but this is not an option. In fact, the more we try to avoid communicating, the more we communicate. We share something by not communicating. Perhaps we are shy, angry, or crying, perhaps too busy. Ignoring someone is communicating with them; we

may not tell them we're ignoring them, but we hope to make that clear through nonverbal communication. Nonverbal communication allows us to communicate far more effectively and honestly than we can with words. Your body posture and position, eye contact (or lack thereof), and the tiniest and most subtle mannerisms are all examples of how you communicate with others. Furthermore, you are constantly communicating with others; you pick up signals from others and interpret them in specific ways, and your ability to understand interpersonal communication depends on your ability to interpret interpersonal communication.

2.2 Words Do Not Remain Your Slave Once You Speak Out

Interpersonal Communication is an irreversible process; you can wish you hadn't said something or apologize for something you said and later regret, but you can't take it back. We frequently act and communicate with others based on previous communication experiences. These encounters may or may not be valuable reference points. We stereotype people, often unconsciously, based on their gender, social status, religion, race, age, and other characteristics—stereotypes are broad generalizations that are frequently exaggerated. Because of stereotypes, when we communicate with others, we may have preconceived notions about what they are thinking and how they are likely to behave, and we may have preconceived notions about the conversation's outcome. These preconceptions influence the way we communicate with others, including the words used and the tone of the voice. We naturally communicate in the manner that we believe is most appropriate for the individual with whom we are

conversing. Unfortunately, our assumptions about others are frequently incorrect. This could indicate that our Communication is ineffective and thus more likely to be misinterpreted. We have failed to communicate because the goal of all Communication is to achieve understanding. By communicating in this manner and being swayed by preconceived notions, we reinforce stereotypes in the person we are conversing with, exacerbating the problem. Commence all interpersonal Communication with an open mind; instead of hearing what you expect to hear, listen to what is being said. There is a very low probability that you will be misunderstood or make statements you later come to regret.

2.3 Endless Complexity

There are many explanations why communication takes place, how it takes place, and how messages are broadcast and received, and no mode of communication is simple. Language, environment, and distraction, as well as the individuals involved in the communication, all have an impact on how messages are sent, received, and interpreted. When we communicate verbally, we swap words that mean different things to different people in different situations. It could be contended that words are nothing more than tokens that we exchange with one another, with no inherent meaning. We can say the same thing to different people, but each of them will have a different interpretation or perception of what we're saying. No matter how minor, any misunderstanding will impact the message that is received at any point during communication.

2.4 Theories of Interpersonal Relationship

The term "interpersonal relationship" refers to a strong bond between people who share similar tastes, goals, and interests in life. Individuals must have a healthy relationship with one another for faster delivery of results and a positive workplace atmosphere. Let us go through the theories of interpersonal relationship development in detail:

Social Exchange Theory

In the year 1958, George Casper Homans proposed the Social Exchange Theory. According to Social Exchange Theory, "give and take" is at the heart of almost all relationships, though the proportions may vary depending on the relationship's intensity. Every person in a relationship has expectations of his or her partner. A relationship that is devoid of expectations is pointless. According to Social Exchange theory, feelings and emotions must be reciprocated for a successful and long-lasting relationship. One-sided relationships are impossible. Only when a person gets something out of a relationship does he invest his time and energy in it. There are times when a person receives less than he gives in a relationship. As a result, the individual begins to compare his connection to that of others. Comparisons can be extremely dangerous because they prevent people from giving their all in relationships. Don't always imagine yourself in a better situation with someone else. Recognize the partner and do everything you can to help him or her. Don't always rely on the other person to take the initiative. Take charge of your destiny and place a high value on your partner.

Uncertainty Reductions Theory

Uncertainty Reductions Theory was proposed by both Charles R. Berger and Richard J. Calabrese to describe the relationship between individuals who do not know each other well or are strangers. According to the Uncertainty Reductions Theory, two strangers meeting for the first time go through a series of steps to reduce their level of uncertainty and become closer. Strangers must communicate effectively to get to know one another and determine their compatibility level. The stages that people go through to reduce the uncertainty level in their relationships are listed below:

Entry Stage

The initial stage is marked by two people getting to know each other better. Each person tries to learn about the other's background, family, educational qualifications, interests, and hobbies, among other things. To strengthen the bond and take the relationship to the next level, each person reveals his or her likes and dislikes.

Personal Stage

Individuals try to learn more about their partner's attitude and beliefs in the second stage, also known as the personal stage. Individuals try to learn more about the other person's ethics, values, behavior, and general nature. In the personal stage, no more strangers learn more about each other's personality traits.

The Exit Stage

The Personal Stage determines the relationship's fate. Individuals who enjoy each other's company decide to make

long-term commitments, such as getting married or staying together indefinitely. Not every relationship blossom into a marriage. Individuals who are unable to understand and adjust to one another decide to end their relationship for the sake of a better future. Individuals exiting relationships in quest of a more compatible partner are said to be in the exit stage.

2.5 Different Types of Interpersonal Relationships

Do you ever consider how many different kinds of relationships you have in your life? What distinguishes one from the other? A healthy relationship could very well develop provided two individuals can connect and align based on core values such as honesty, respect, communication, accountability, and loyalty, regardless of the type of relationship. But the thing is, you can nurture each kind of relationship you form differently. A relationship begins when two people feel at ease in each other's company and decide to spend time together. Interpersonal relationship refers to a close bond between people who have similar interests and goals. Interpersonal relationships are formed by people who are compatible with one another. For a healthy and robust relationship, people must get along well. Let's take a look at the different types of interpersonal relationships:

Family Relationship

A family is defined as a group of people who are related by blood or marriage. Parents, siblings, grandparents, aunts, spouses, children, uncles, cousins, and other relatives make up the family. These people influence both your physical and mental development and show you what relationships are like, especially from a young age. Consider some of your life's firsts:

- Learning to ride a bike
- Getting your first family pet
- Graduating from high school

Consider those historic moments. Then try to recall which of the relatives were present in those moments. That's right, your loved ones. As you get older, you'll notice that family relationships, through family rules and traditions, help form your backbone and make you who you are. But not every family relationship is perfect; we all know there are ups and downs. However, as you grow older, you'll be looking for signs of faith, communication, and dependability.

Most importantly, you will try to work together to resolve conflict to describe a healthy family relationship. Togetherness is important because, regardless of the good or bad times, you are encouraging ways to grow and strengthen bonds, which is what makes a family so robust. Our family, also known as relatives, are people with whom we share some form of kinships, such as blood (as with brothers, parents, and sisters), marriage (as with non-blood uncles and aunts or stepparents), romantic relationships (as with a parent's boyfriend or girlfriend), or adoption. Family members include siblings and parents, whom you may see every day as a child, as well as cousins, aunts, uncles, and grandparents, whom you may not see as often. Families come in various shapes and sizes, including single-parent families, stepfamilies, and homes with gay and lesbian parents. People should, in theory, have strong bonds with their families, but this does not always take place. They should feel loved and close to their relatives, and they should be able to confide in them and talk about personal matters with them. Parents, as well as older relatives play a primary role in providing guidance and support. Whenever deemed necessary, parents and relatives set for you the boundaries and discipline. Arguments and disagreements can arise because families are so close and spend so much time together, but they are usually short-lived in most families, and even in emotional outbursts or hurt, families still love and care about each other. Family relationships should ideally last a lifetime, though as children grow into teenagers and then adults, they typically gain more independence, and the parental relationship shifts from one of guidance to one of mutual support. As children grow into teenagers and adults, they may have more disagreements and conflicts with their parents as they try to demonstrate their independence and find their adult identity. This is entirely normal, and it usually subsides once the adolescent years have passed. It is critical to maintaining open communication lines with family members because a family can provide lifelong support if a healthy relationship is cultivated. The ability to form other types of relationships outside of the family unit, like friendships and romantic relationships, is influenced by one's relationship with one's family. In some families, there is little physical contact, whereas in others, kissing on the cheek or forehead, hugging, patting the head or tousling the hair, patting on the back, and so on are common ways for family members to express affection. Carrying or holding babies as well as younger children are typical.

Friendship

Friends are people with whom we choose to interact despite not being related. Friends are people whom we trust, regard, and care about and with whom we feel comfortable confiding and spending time. Honesty, support, and loyalty should be the foundations of any good friendship. A friendship is a two-way street; both people must see each other as friends for it to exist. Friendship comes in various degrees. You may discover that you have a stronger bond with some friends than others. This is completely natural. Some friends may not be suitable to confide in about personal issues or concerns, especially if they have only known you for a brief period or are not seen very often. You may find that you are more comfortable and able to confide in friends with whom you have spent more time or have known for a longer period. Best friends are friends who are extremely close as well as know each other exceptionally well. Some people have a large number of friends, while others have only a few. There is no such thing as the "right" or "wrong" number of friends, and everyone is different. Friendships that are mutually respectful, supportive, and share common interests and ideas are considered good. While some friendships are close and friends welcome each other by hugging or kissing on the cheek, others have no physical contact or simply shake hands. In a friendship, physical intimacy or romantic touch is not appropriate. Friendship is a type of unconditional interpersonal relationship that people enter into of their own free will. Friendship is a type of relationship in which there are no formalities, and people enjoy being in each other's company. Friendship can exist between:

- A man and a woman.
- A man and a man.
- A woman and a woman.

Friendships are the kinds of relationships that come and go throughout a person's life. It's fine if we don't have the same friends now as we did when we were younger. Individuals grow and change as they grow older, which is a healthy and natural part of life. As a result, friendships are expected to follow suit. Because friends are the people you choose, your friendship with them is built on similar core values as your relationship with the family. Healthy friendships allow you to give and receive the same kind of support which keeps you honest, confident,

and motivated. And while it may appear that knowing and socializing with a large number of people is all that is required to have great friendships, you should always consider how those friendships make you feel. Friendship is a two-way street.

Consequently, when you accept someone for what they are and show genuine interest in their life and well-being, and if they can reciprocate, you've made a friend. Friendships exist to serve as an extension of your support system, guiding you through both good and bad times. Friendships can bring great fulfillment to life and overall well-being, whether you need a shoulder to cry on or someone to share exciting news with.

What Is Imperative in a Friendship?

Transparency is the most important factor in maintaining a long-term friendship. Don't keep secrets from your friends. Tell them the truth. When necessary, they will be guided. Never give them bad advice or suggestions. Ego, jealousy, hatred, and anger are not present in friendship. The entire friendship relationship is built on trust and reciprocity. No relationship, including friendship, can be one-sided. Try to help your friends as much as you can. Love is a term used to describe an interpersonal relationship marked by passion, intimacy, trust, and respect. A romantic relationship involves two people who have strongly connected as well as share a strong bond.

Romantic Relationship

A romantic relationship is a relationship in which you are strongly attracted to the other person's personality and physical appearance. The other person in the relationship reciprocates this. A romantic relationship is when a boyfriend and girlfriend-in a heterosexual relationship- or a boyfriend and boyfriend-in a homosexual relationship- or spouses (in a marriage) or life

partners are involved in a civil partnership or long-term unmarried relationship. People in a romantic relationship can be together frequently, and when they are apart, they will frequently communicate, such as by phone. Some people who are in romantic relationships share a home. A romantic relationship is the most intimate type of relationship, and the two people involved would then frequently describe themselves as "attracted to" or "in love." They have an intense bond with each other that they don't have with anybody else, even close friends, and it's exclusive and monogamous. Love, respect, acceptance, trust, support, shared interests, and an inclination for the 2 people involved to share their lives are the foundations of romantic relationships. Some people in relationships may want to start a family. Because it's such a close relationship, various forms of physical contact are tolerated that would be inappropriate in any other situation. Long-term cuddling and holding, kissing on the lips, and sexual intercourse are examples, but they should all be mutually agreed upon. In romantic relationships, disagreements and arguments do arise from time to time. These arguments can be overcome in strong relationships through effective communication, understanding, and compromise, but in other cases, particularly if there are frequent arguments, the two people involved may decide to end the relationship. Relationships can last for a long time or a short time. Some relationships end after only a few months because it becomes clear that the two people involved are not compatible and do not want to spend their lives together. In other cases, the two people may have been together for many years or even their entire lives. In this relationship, both partners must have faith in each other. Respect and admiration for one another are essential. For the charm to remain in the relationship for a longer period, partners must reciprocate each other's feelings. When two people in love intend to take the relationship to the next level, they marry. Marriage is a type of formalized relationship in which two people who have known each other for a long time decide to marry and stay together through thick and thin. Understanding, love, passion, intimacy, respect, and trust are the keys to a successful marriage. Even if two people love each other, they may decide not to marry. They're frequently referred to as boyfriend and girlfriend. They might or might not be able to stay together. They are said to be in a live-in relationship if they stay together without getting married. Long-distance relationships refer to people who are in a relationship but live in different locations. Individuals who are having difficulty getting along may decide to end their relationship to have a better future. Following up on Valentine's Day, the last topic I'd like to discuss is romantic relationships, which can often appear to be the most complicated. What is the reason for this? It's made up of several different components, to be sure. Passion, emotional commitment, and intimacy are all factors in the romantic relationships we have in our lives. Let's not forget about love, that powerful four-letter word that can elevate a relationship to new heights. On the other hand, a romantic relationship necessitates mutual trust and time to develop and ongoing effort. This happens over time as you learn to relax and let go of your guard, becoming as satisfied with another person as you are with yourself. You'll be able to share your deepest thoughts and emotions without fear of being judged by the other person. Then there's the desire to be physically embraced by a partner: kissing, hugging, holding hands, intimacy, and so on. A romantic relationship's layers can become so thick that the deeper you peel back, the more committed you become to the other person. You must also consider love languages, which are the various ways each of us desires and expresses love. Did you know there are five different types of love languages? Some people are looking for quality time or gifts. Some people require affirmation in the form of words or physical touch. On the other hand, some people prefer acts of service, such as doing something helpful for the partner. And, as you can see, the layers of understanding a romantic relationship or your partner are the reasons why these kinds of relationships can feel difficult. But one thing to keep in mind is that you must first love yourself. The love you give yourself has a huge impact on the various relationships you have in your life. It assists you in making healthy decisions for your overall well-being and determining what is in your best interests. Don't be afraid to show yourself the love you deserve by loving yourself more deeply. This is the first step toward manifesting a loving, passionate, and completely unbreakable bond in a current or future relationship.

Platonic Relationship

A platonic relationship is defined as a relationship between two people who have no feelings or sexual attraction for each other. A man and a woman are just friends in such a relationship, and they do not mix love and friendship.

Platonic relationships may develop into romantic relationships as both partners develop mutual love and fall in love with one another.

Professional Relationship (Work Relationship)

A professional relationship is defined as a group of people who work for the same company. Colleagues are people with whom you have a professional relationship. Colleagues might or might not get along.

Acquaintanceships

Acquaintances are individuals you may run into regularly but who are not family or friends. They could be a neighbor who lives down the street from you and whom you greet whenever you see them, a work colleague, or someone you've met a few times at a social event but don't know well. It is critical to treat acquaintances with politeness and respect, as having mutually beneficial relationships with people around you, like coworkers, college classmates, neighbors, and others is a critical way to avoid stress and conflict. Relationships that begin as acquaintanceships may evolve into friendships over time as you get to know the person effectively and see them more often. The amount of contact with a friend is minimal. There is a very low probability of any physical contact (although you may be required to shake hands in a work setting or when introduced to someone) but smiling and saying 'hello' will most likely be the main form of contact. An acquaintance is similar to a friend in that they are people you know but not a friend. This could be a classmate, coworker, or even a mutual friend. Affiliations can be thought of as more casual friendships that serve to establish connections, obtain references, or simply see people regularly, such as at the coffee shop or gym. Acquaintances, like the people in your community, are usually a more diverse group of people because they communicate with a much broader set of social networks, unlike our close friends. If you don't know someone personally or haven't had any intentional social encounters, chances are they are your acquaintance. It's perfectly normal for us to have more acquaintances as compared to close friends. The advantage is that we can expand our network by sparking connections between others. So, even just a little social interaction with acquaintances in your neighborhood or at the gym can help you feel more connected.

2.6 Role of Employees in Interpersonal Relationship Development

Individuals must get along with their coworkers to maintain a positive work environment and maintain healthy interpersonal relationships. Individuals must trust one another at work to have better working relationships. Working alone is nearly impossible for employees. Everyone requires the company of others to discuss issues and find better solutions. Let's take a look at how employees play a role in interpersonal relationships.

Show Positive Behavior

Employees must maintain a positive attitude at work. Do not always look for flaws in your coworkers. Keep in mind that no one on this planet is perfect. Irrespective of how wrong the other person is, one must maintain the workplace's decorum. Instead of indulging in conflicts and sabotaging relationships, the right approach ignores the one you don't like. Friends become foes when they are involved in a row.

Flexibility

Employees will need to adjust a little more. Things aren't always going to be the way you want them to be. Listening to others and trying to understand what they're saying will be beneficial. Don't consider protecting personal interests all of the time.

Do Not Berate Co-workers

Never underestimate the value of your coworkers. You never know when someone will think of something brilliant. Everyone should be treated with respect. Ignoring people causes

frustration and, as a result, ruins relationships at work. Everyone should be heard. Employees are irritated when only a few people are given priority while others are ignored. Employees are de-motivated to give their best when they are faced with such situations. They begin to view the office as well as work as a source of stress.

Stay Away from Biased Approach

Never show favoritism to anyone. Employees who perform well should be recognized in front of their peers. Those who fail to meet expectations should be asked to pull their socks up the next time, regardless of their relationship with you or senior management. Even if one of your team members is your best friend, he should not be spared when it comes to results and targets. Work and personal relationships should never be mixed.

Avoid Rumormongering

Spreading rumors inside the workplace is unethical. Backbiting, leg-pulling, and criticism are the most common causes of employee dissatisfaction. Learn to be honest with yourself. If you believe a colleague is misbehaving, tell him directly rather than discussing it with others. It is unprofessional to make fun of others.

Establish Trust

A person should be trustworthy. If one of your coworkers has confided in you about something, do not betray him. Do not approach your boss and divulge all of his secrets. Learn to keep your mouth closed.

Arrogance Destroys Everything

Avoid being conceited. Showing an unnecessary attitude to those around you is not a good idea. You may be the head of a department, but that does not give you the legitimacy to be rude to those around you. You are being compensated for your services, and no one will put up with your domineering and bossy demeanor. When you walk into your office, leave your ego at the door.

Weigh Your Words Before Talking

Think before you speak. You have to ensure that your words do not hurt people. You should never humiliate or insult anyone intentionally.

Be Nice to Everyone

Greet your coworkers, even if they are not on your team. It doesn't really matter. A simple smile can make a huge difference.

2.7 Types of Marital Relationships

According to the latest study carried out by the University of Illinois, marital relationships can be divided into four categories. A total of 376 couples were surveyed, and they were asked to keep a detailed record of how committed they felt to their partner. While there were some outliers, experts concluded that there were four different couple types.

The Dramatic Couple

In the study, this is the most popular type of couple. Throughout the relationship, the partners undergo the most changes in their level of commitment. The individuals who were in dramatic relationships had the lowest levels of emotional intimacy of any of the study's groups. When we converse about drama queens, relationship drama, drama kings, or other dramatic people in a relationship, we're talking about the emotional upheaval or turbulence in a relationship on an episodic level and has no resolution. In simple terms, it's an emotional state in which one or both partners in a relationship manipulate and control each other to create an unpleasant feeling. Drama refers to fabricated conflict. You typically fight just for the sake of fighting in a debate where there's no actual conversation. A lack of authenticity in an engagement can also be a source of relationship drama. For example, it's rarely about the other person when you yell at the partner (for whatever reason). The lack of authenticity arises from your lack of understanding of the problem, and you begin blaming your partner through manipulation, control, or anger-based behaviors.

How does a relationship drama look like in real life?
In a dramatic situation, it often appears that a past event has occurred again. You might, for instance, leave the dirty socks on the floor each day, and the partner will take them to the laundry hamper. If your partner, rather than having a conversation with you about the socks or leaving the socks be, begins shouting at you in public about the socks, a drama may ensue. "Isn't it possible for you to ever clean up after yourself? What kind of individual do you believe I am? Isn't it true that I'm just your maid? What's the matter with you!?"There is no doubt

that when we're not in the moment, this reaction appears absurd and unjustified. Yet, when we're in the midst of a tumultuous relationship, we rarely notice that our own actions are also tumultuous.

How to avoid relationship drama?
So, how do we get rid of drama in our lives when it's so hard to realize we're doing it at the moment? We must be self-assured and love ourselves. Of course, this isn't the most straightforward task. In the case of the dirty socks, the person shouting about them would have to examine his feelings and why the

socks are so important that he warrants such a public outburst. Is it true that it's all about the socks? To avoid drama, the irritated partner will need to take a breath and figure out why the socks are bothering them in the first place. Do they feel neglected, unappreciated, or exploited? It will come down to a person's belief in every situation.

The Conflicted Couple

While conflicted couples have more passionate love, they also have more fights than the other couples on this list. These couples have few shared interests and spend less free time together than the time they spend with their friends. A disagreement in a relationship can be defined as any disagreement, such as an argument or an ongoing series of disagreements, such as over money. Conflict can be nerve-wracking, but it can also help to "clear the air," bringing up issues that need to be addressed. We may become enraged due to conflicts and disagreements, or we may become enraged as a result of something else. At work, we might try to keep our tempers in check and stop saying things we'll come to regret later. Unfortunately, we are more likely to say hurtful

things to others at home as a result of this. There are also fewer people around who can mediate, so disagreements can escalate quickly in a way that does not occur at work. As a result, conflict in a relationship can quickly escalate into something both unpleasant and personal. Unfortunately, when we are connected to someone, we often know how to hurt them the most. That may be precisely what we intend to do in anger, no matter how much we regret it later. Denial, smoothing over, or fighting are all options for many people. However, the problem with this is that these are not long-term solutions to the problem. They're only covering up the flaws, which isn't feasible in a long-term relationship or. Rather, the relationship is unlikely to prove long-term if this is the chosen approach. In general, honest communication about feelings, particularly feelings about something being wrong, will always work better in a romantic relationship. Moving beyond those three to compromise or, better yet, collaboration is the key to a successful relationship. In a compromise, you each give up something in exchange for an agreed-upon middle ground. The said is more likely to produce a positive outcome than win/lose, but it isn't quite a win/win. Because you both gave up something, neither of you is likely to be significantly satisfied with the outcome, which could lead to you revisiting the subject again and again. When you work collaboratively, you work together to create a win-win situation by leveraging your differences. It takes time, but it is worth the effort in a relationship.

How to move towards collaboration

Of course, the big question is how to move from fighting to collaboration, especially if you've already established a fighting pattern. A few suggestions are as follows:

You have to learn to talk before getting angry as well as work out a strategy

Conflict resolution necessitates commitment from both parties. Discuss how you want to handle disagreements ahead of time and decide that you will support each other in doing so. You might find it beneficial to talk about how you act when you're angry and support each other in managing your emotions. If one of you becomes enraged quickly, for example, the other may find it helpful to suggest that you talk later.

Walk away when you are angry

Make it a habit to avoid discussing problems when you're angry. Say something like, "I can't talk right now because I'm too angry." Please wait until I've calmed down before we discuss this." Then walk away and find a quiet place to relax.

You must not try to discuss complex issues when you are tired or are hungry

When we are tired or hungry, we are more likely to be depressed and difficult. It's in our nature. You must stay away from indulging in difficult conversations when you're in a bad mood. Instead, choose a time when you are both comfortable and relaxed, and your exchanges will be less likely to turn into a fight. Some people prefer to go for a walk, while others prefer to spend time at home: experiment and see what works the best for you.

You should be ready to apologize

You may believe that you were correct. You might even have been right. Being willing to apologize for your partner's feelings, on the other hand, will go a long way toward ensuring that they feel heard and that you understand their concerns. This is especially true if you ended up yelling at each other despite your best intentions. When you apologize, it does not mean that you are accepting your mistake. It entails expressing regret for the disagreement and remorse for your partner's distress and a commitment to finding a solution that benefits both of you.

Listen and discuss

Prepare to pay attention to your partner. Don't just explain your viewpoint over and over, or you'll end up fighting again. Establishing a compromise and a collaborative solution necessitates a thorough understanding of what is important to them and why. Moreover, it is also imperative to indulge in a constructive exchange of viewpoints and opinions.

The Social Couple

These couples frequently share friendships and social networks. In comparison to other couples, their love is more "friendship-based." Sociable couples share a lot of interests and are heavily influenced by social media.

The Partner-Focused Couple

Out of the four types of couples, partner-focused couples manifest the highest possible level of relationship satisfaction. They spend a lot of their free time together and have a lot of

similar interests. Partner-focused couples are the most committed of all relationship types and are the most likely to marry.

Interpersonal relationships that help you to succeed in business world

Relationships in your life can either propel your business to new heights of success or make you want to give up entrepreneurship altogether. We frequently struggle in our businesses and other areas of our lives, and we fail to connect the dots between what's going on in our personal lives and what's going on in our professional lives. We miss a problem that is right in front of our eyes. Each of the many types of relationships we have in our lives impacts our level of business success. To be successful, you must first comprehend these relationships and then learn how to deal with situations that may later become roadblocks. Given below are the four major types of relationships that can affect your business positively or negatively.

Romantic Relationships

Although this is not the essential type of relationship in your business, it has the biggest influence on your attitude and mindset. Each of us wishes to spend our lives with someone we adore, and love is an emotion that can take you on a roller coaster ride. It's critical to find a romantic partner who gets you and understands what it's like to be with an entrepreneur. Entrepreneurship is not for everyone, and it has shattered several relationships along the way. If you're with someone who doesn't get it, their attitude can impact how much time you spend working and how you appear to the customers mentally, emotionally, and physically.

Friendships

Friends who care about you will encourage you and help you achieve your goals. Bad friends try to bring you down to their level. They can't see beyond their immediate circumstances, so they generalize and assume it's the same for everyone. You've probably heard a lot of quotes about how the people with whom you associate can influence your life. As an entrepreneur, your goal should be to be surrounded by people who are making changes in their lives. They're working hard to get ahead, and they're looking to interconnect with other like-minded business owners. Those are the kinds of friends who will aid in the expansion of your company.

Business Partnerships

"The only ship that won't sail is a partnership," Dave Ramsey famously said. He is a firm believer in avoiding business partnerships because they are tough to maintain. There is no guarantee that Dave Ramsey is correct, but any partnership necessitates constant effort, honesty, communication, and a variety of other factors to succeed. When forming partnerships, you, like your friends, must be strategic and patient. Many opportunities will appear to be beneficial to your business, but they may be harmful. Even if you know the person, you must research them. It is better than before entering a business partnership; you must obtain clarity—especially legally. Choose wisely since your business performance may be at stake and dependent on the proposed partnership.

Fans, Followers, and Clients

The final type of relationship is the one that will develop over time but remains crucial. Word-of-mouth marketing will kick in as you create value in your market, and your business will grow. Your business will increase as you add more value and assist people with their most pressing issues. Those in your world will be watching you and paying attention to what you do. This has both positive and negative aspects. Time will be a significant challenge for you. Your fans, followers, and clients will demand more of your time to get answers to their questions or simply to get your perspective. Because time is the one resource you cannot replace, you will be forced to say no more. You risk upsetting some people by doing so, but the reality is that you can't please everyone. Maintaining control is crucial in this type of relationship. This is your life and your company. In your life, you will have many different kinds of relationships. The key is to comprehend them and prevent them from negatively impacting your business. For every adverse scenario mentioned above, there is a possibility that the opposite is true. Relationships can help you grow as well as focus on the things that will help your company succeed. It is up to you to decide what effect they have on your business. It is recommended that you always make informed decisions.

Chapter 3
Carl Rogers and Happy Relationships

Though it is challenging yet it is not impossible to establish good relationships provided you work on the following:

- How to deal with change in your relationship
- How to react what not to do in a crisis
- How to make the relationships work for you daily in every possible way
- Learn how to improve your relationships to be happier, healthier, and live longer
- Make sure your relationships pay off in terms of peace, love, and happiness
- How to deal with and resolve relationship issues
- Make love stronger as well as more resilient for it to withstand the test of time
- How to cope with relationships that aren't as common as others
- How to stay out of toxic relationships
- When others tend to defer it or avoid saying what needs to be said, learn to communicate

Relationships evolve with time. They're living, breathing arrangements that are constantly changing. As people get older, their relationship partners change. Change, on the other hand, is frightening in all kinds of relationships. Nevertheless, a good relationship can withstand the test of time and improve over time, becoming more valuable and desirable as it overcomes its setbacks and problems. This is only possible if you prioritize your relationship and both partners are constantly growing and improving to become successful partners. As a result, the relationship never feels stale, and it always feels youthful and new. We are happier and healthier when we have good relationships. Ignoring a good relationship is the best way to ruin it. When you think everything is fine and become preoccupied with other things, your relationship can quickly become jeopardized. Relationships can change in unfavorable ways and surprise you, mainly if you haven't discovered how to cultivate and manage them. It is beneficial to keep the beloved relationships in good working order and never to let them go. Learning practical relationship skills and building a toolbox of relationship methods and techniques pays off. Our connections are intertwined and grow into a rich tapestry of lovely threads. We achieve peace of mind when we establish good, healthy relationships in all aspects of our lives. Successful relationships provide meaning, grace, and joy to our lives. Relationships can shift in unexpected ways, throwing us off balance. What is your opinion of the quality of your relationships? Would you give a high score to your professional relationships but a low score to your family relationships? Or do you consider your family relationships to be excellent but romantic relationships to be wrong? You may need to recognize weak areas and work on improving them to live the happiest life possible. If your relationship with yourself, for example, is strained, you'll need to work on improving your self-trust, self-confidence, and self-talk. For you, self-improvement would be a top priority. What is the reason for this? Because the relationship affects you; as a result, it affects all of your other relationships. All of your relationships will be influenced by your relationship with yourself. It is the foundation of your existence. Ask yourself how you feel about yourself, if you are at ease in your skin, and know who you are?

3.1 Happy Relationships

Strong, healthy relationships are the foundation of a happy life. Everyone wants to be in happy relationships that would last a lifetime. Long-lasting friendships and mutually beneficial associations that bring us joy for a lifetime are so glad relationships.

Carl Rogers' Formula

Building great relationships becomes a reality if we try to emulate Carl Rogers' three precepts of empathy, congruence, and unconditional positive regard. Rogers' advice can be followed by constantly attempting to be empathic, understanding, as well as sympathetic toward the person with whom you are dealing, communicating honestly and truthfully, and providing unconditional care and concern.

3.2 How to Win with Your Relationships?

If you follow the tips and suggestions listed below in all of your relationships, business or personal, you will be successful in making all your relationships happier.

Passionate Relationships

Love sizzles in passionate relationships. They make you feel as if you're floating above your problems. Our brains sizzle when we're in emotional relationships. When we are in love or passionate, our brains are stimulated more. Although there can be conflict and problems in passionate relationships, they are very beneficial to both partners. It appears to be much easier to solve problems in a good relationship than in a bad one. Everyone is clamoring for more of the beautiful stuff. It's similar to desire fuel. It makes us eagerly anticipate each moment and inspires us to live life to the fullest.

How to Make Relationships More Passionate?

To begin, it is always beneficial if each partner in a relationship is passionate about his or her own life. Every day starts with your energizing smile if you are passionate about your life. Others in your life pick up on the energy and want to be around you. You will bring a lot of positive energy into the relationships if you are passionate about your job. This could have a powerful positive impact on the most important relationships. The ties will percolate when each person is energized by their work and feels a sense of fulfillment because they are doing something they passionately believe in. We have a sense of mission and purpose in our lives when we view our work as a labor of love. And we operate with a high degree of consistency. Our lives are organized around a real plan, and we're doing things for a reason, a good cause, something we believe in. We adore it and are highly enthusiastic about it. If you are dissatisfied with your current job, the simple solution is to seek out more fulfilling work, something about which you can be truly passionate. Something you strongly believe in or feel called to do. However, you may feel enslaved in a job that will

never make you happy. If that's the case, it's time to make a change. People don't always want to hear that. They believe it is too much work or that they are too old to pursue another career path. I've discovered that it's rarely too late. Relationships are similar to careers. You can start by revisiting your values and doing more of what matters to you. You can stoke the fires of desire by strengthening your friendship and bond. You can concentrate on the positive aspects of your relationship and build on its strengths. Positive thought and action can inspire you to feel and act in brave and new ways.

Passionate Relationships and Romance

People in passionate relationships sometimes seek lust or enchantment rather than passion. They want dynamic relationships to be defined by the euphoria that often occurs in the initial two or three years of a new relationship. Mature relationships go through stages and changes, and the couple settles into a quieter, maybe more peaceful way of being together after moving past the enchantment phase. If the couple could indeed stop and appreciate the warm glow that comes with knowing and loving each other ever so deeply, it can be even more gorgeous than the enchantment phase. Relationships that have matured can be like fine wine. The distinction is subtle but also very satisfying. Take the time to search for as well as cultivate those subtleties.

3.3 Work Relationships

Using the fundamentals of Carl Rogers's theory of human relations and his counseling approach, you can have successful, productive, and satisfying work relationships. The American Psychological Association named Rogers the twentieth-century psychologist shortly before his death. His ideas inspired people from all walks of life, and he taught professional helpers all over the world how to serve people in the most effective way possible. Whatever you want to achieve, you'll need the help as well as the cooperation of others to get it done, whether you want to:

- Supervise, direct or lead people
- Get a new job
- Enhance the income or wealth
- Improve the happiness level or peace of mind
- Expand the spiritual awareness
- Enhance your athletic performance

Workplace relationships are the cornerstone of any career's success. It will be critical to know the right people and establish successful relationships. Your ability to succeed will be determined by your relationships with coworkers, mentors, coaches, and supervisors. Carl Rogers' ideas and techniques will assist you in commanding great respect from others and forming meaningful friendships and alliances. You must not only know people, but you must also maintain your presence in their presence. This entails keeping relationships with valuable customers or potential customers, allies, and referral sources through networking. The strength of any network is determined by the quality of one's relationships with the people in one's address book. Assume you haven't spoken to someone in months or even years. Then one day, you'll require his assistance. When you call him, you learn that he has moved or is no longer in the same line of work and is not interested in the services. He or she may no longer have the same level of trust in you and will no longer be able to support you because you ended the relationship. You've allowed yourself to fade away from his radar. He probably thinks you didn't value the relationship enough.

Achieving Success in Work Relationships

It's simple to remain in the minds of the customers, contacts, and other vital relationships' minds. Roger's three helpful fundamentals can help you develop and strengthen your critical work relationships. To form successful relationships, Rogers suggested that a practical helper should have three qualities:

Empathy

It would enable her to gain the person's trust while also allowing the counselor to demonstrate his genuine concern for the individual.

Congruence

It entails being genuine and honest with the client, being one's true self, and not playing games or employing gimmicks.

Unconditional Positive Regard

It demonstrates genuine concern and care, as well as nonjudgmental acceptance of her. It shows that the person will not be rejected or abandoned by the helper for any reason. What possibilities might arise if you applied the three principles to everyone in your life?

- You'd be a well-known and respected figure
- You'd form plenty of rewarding and fruitful relationships

- You'd show authentic leadership
- You'd also increase your worth to the people you know
- You'd earn their love and appreciation, as well as valuable assistance as and when you need it

Your initiatives, as well as projects, would receive a lot of support. People will come to your aid because they know you, trust you, and know you will always be there for them.

It appears to be a simple task, but many people overlook it. Even though most of us are acquainted with these concepts today, many leaders have wholly overlooked how to apply them to their daily work. However, they were groundbreaking ideas at the time of Rogers. Although we are aware of concepts, we do not always apply them to our professional relationships. Suppose we have the wisdom to set aside a little time to apply these ideas to various situations and enhance the quality of excellence of a state-of-the-art networking plan. In that case, we can use them in all our relationships.

Building Great Work Relationships Is Exciting

Being open and honest with someone we're just beginning to know can take a lot of guts. To seek a rich, fulfilling work connection with someone, takes a genuine desire. We need to be able to show empathy and support to others, especially if we don't share much in common. We want to continue to establish strong connections based on unconditional positive regard. Nonetheless, forming a new friendship or transforming a stranger into a strong ally is hugely fulfilling and exhilarating. Successful people treat everyone with respect and provide high-quality service. Giving and caring is an integral part of demonstrating authentic leadership through our interactions. The Carl Rogers technique is the best way to provide leadership and maintain solid relationships. It usually guarantees your long-term prosperity as well as happiness. In time, what you give to others will come back to you tenfold.

3.4 Essential Elements for Developing a Healthy Relationship

It is essential to differentiate between a healthy as well as an unhealthy relationship. Healthy connections make you feel good and lift you, whereas toxic connections make you feel bad and might even make you miserable. Everyone deserves to be in a happy, healthy relationship, and with the proper partner at their side, this is possible. The essentials for establishing a healthy relationship are outlined here.

Communication

You have probably heard the overused phrase "communication is important." But here's the thing: there's a reason it's a cliché.

One of the most critical parts of establishing a good relationship is good communication. It is crucial to talk about what you want and anticipate when starting a new relationship. This may include being open and honest about complex topics, but if you are in a healthy relationship, your spouse will be receptive as well as listen.

Moreover, you should also reciprocate accordingly. Being on the same page as the partner goes a long way, and it's equally vital to open up to the partner about what's hurting you, compromise over arguments, and appreciate each other. While communication is essential, you both should be comfortable with the frequency with which you communicate with one another. It's not good if your partner expects you to respond immediately and text them all day if you don't want to. On the other hand, if your partner consistently ignores the texts and makes you feel bad, it isn't healthy. It's critical to strike a communication balance which you and your partner are both happy with.

Respect

Listening to your partner (not just waiting for them to talk) and understanding their point of view is an essential approach to demonstrating respect in the relationship. Respect your partner's choices and beliefs, even if you disagree about who should be the next president or whether you're Team Taylor or they're Team Kimye. Try not to convince them to change their minds on things that matter to them, such as studying abroad for a semester and where they want to reside after graduation. Both parties in a happy relationship will have mutual regard for one another. Simply because you don't always agree, it doesn't mean one of you has to change their views for the relationship to work. Respect for your partner's privacy and limits is another important aspect of establishing respect in a relationship. You

don't have the right to know everything your partner does or who they communicate with. It also entails being aware of your partner's feelings and refraining from doing things that may cause them significant pain, such as keeping things between you two that are supposed to be private. Knowing each other's passwords and seeing the pink heart emoji next to their names in Snapchat aren't indicators of a good relationship. While sharing those things is fine, healthy relationships necessitate some distance and a filter.

Boundaries

We all have our boundaries in terms of what makes us feel good, secure, and safe. You should feel 100 percent comfortable communicating such limits in a healthy relationship and trust that they will be respected, and the same applies to your partner. It's fine if you only want to hang out three times a week. It's ok if you want to wait before becoming personal; if you would like to keep the Monday Fun Day night with the baffles, go ahead. Remember that setting personal limits in any relationship should not be a source of anxiety or fear. It's also important to reevaluate your relationship if you feel that your spouse or friend is using limits to control you, such as instructing you not to hang out with people or demanding you share passwords.

Trust

This is an important issue. Mutual and unrestrained trust between partners is required in all healthy partnerships. Irrespective of what either partner has gone through in the past, such as a parent's divorce or a cheating ex, the partner will trust you entirely in a healthy relationship. Do keep in mind that building trust in a relationship takes time (it seldom happens overnight) and that when your spouse fully believes in you with his or her feelings, you must respect him or her and not betray the trust. It's not right to cheat on someone or do things to make them envious.

On the other hand, you should not be with your partner if you do not trust them. Never allow the partner to use the lack of trust or previous experiences to manipulate you, question you, or make you feel like you have to go out of your way to win their trust. Your relationship's trust will naturally be strengthened by consistent support, affection, respect, and communication.

Support

Having a supportive spouse who you know has your back is one of the most admirable aspects of a happy relationship. In a healthy relationship, you and your partner would support each other and treat each other as equals, whether it's standing up for you when someone says something hurtful about you or always being the rock, you can count on. Your companion will not use strategies to manipulate, control, or humiliate you. They will be watchful of you, but not excessively so. They will motivate you to spend time with family and friends, work toward your objectives, and live a life separate from your partnership. Supportive partners will always choose the best for you and will not prevent you from accomplishing your goals. In a successful relationship, you'll feel like yourself and won't feel obligated to alter or make significant compromises for the relationship to succeed.

3.5 What Isn't Healthy?

An unhealthy relationship is ultimately built on power and control rather than love and respect. If you believe your partner is employing strategies to control you, this is a major red flag, and you should get assistance. It is not necessary for your partner to physically harm you for your relationship to be abusive. It's no good if your relationship is excellent most of the time yet unhealthy on certain occasions. There is never an excuse for abuse, and everyone deserves to be in a healthy relationship. There are no excuses for abusive behavior, even if you have a history of mental illness, cheating, or other difficulties in or outside of your current relationship. It's also important to understand that you can't choose your mate. If you are in an abusive relationship, you should seek treatment immediately rather than waiting for your partner to change his approach and attitude.

Chapter 4
Non-Verbal Communication and Relationships

When we speak of communication, we frequently refer to what we say or the words we use. On the other hand, interpersonal communication is much more than the literal meaning of words and the information or message they communicate. It also includes nonverbal behaviors that convey implicit messages, whether they are deliberate or not. We all know that the hallmarks of a loving relationship are love, trust, and commitment. But how do we cultivate these characteristics? Many of us overlook the importance of communication in developing these qualities. Nonverbal communication is an important aspect of forming connections.

Furthermore, communication is much more than just words. In the 1950s, renowned researcher Albert Mehrabian determined that only around 7% of our message is communicated by the words we speak. While the way we talk accounts for 38% of the message (i.e., the tone of our voice, inflections, and other sounds). The remaining 55% is nonverbal. Facial expressions, voice tone and pitch, body language gestures (kinesics), and physical space between communicators are all examples of nonverbal communication (proxemics). Over and above spoken (verbal) communication, nonverbal signals can provide insights and additional information and meaning.

Simply put, nonverbal communication refers to the nonverbal messages we convey to one another. Without them saying anything, we can tell a lot about how people feel if they're honest with us and what kind of mood they're in. Nonverbal communication includes making and maintaining eye contact, facial expressions, and body motions. We must recognize that nonverbal communication has a significant part in feelings of security and building a sense of connection and affection in marriage and relationships. These signs indicate how we feel to one another: a light, passionate touch, a warm smile with warmth in the eyes, and unconscious transparency in body gestures towards the other person. These kinds of exchanges are crucial in how two individuals in a relationship communicate with one another. Some of us may be unaware of how important nonverbal communication is in our relationships.

4.1 Understanding Nonverbal Communication

Nonverbal communication is important in our lives because it improves a person's capacity to relate, participate, and form meaningful interactions in daily life. People may create deeper relationships with others if they have a better knowledge of this form of communication. Nonverbal communication, often known as body language, can take numerous forms and be received differently by various people, particularly across

cultures. Even the absence of such nonverbal clues can be significant and constitute nonverbal communication in and of itself. Each movement and the combination of motions of the body, such as changes in posture, eye direction, limb gestures, and facial expressions, send signals to others. These signs might be subtle or overt, as well as contradictory: A person's words may communicate one meaning, but their body language may send an entirely another impression. This is particularly true when someone isn't telling the truth. Nonverbal communication is more informative of a person's actual feelings because it is often instinctive and brutal to fake.

4.2 Using Non-Verbal Communication

The process of transmitting a message, sentiment, or concept through physical movements, posture, and facial expressions is known as nonverbal communication. People can benefit from nonverbal communication in the following ways:

Try to Modify What Is Being Said in Words

For example, when saying "Yes," people may firmly nod their heads to show that they concur with the other person. When saying "I'm alright, thanks," a shrug of the shoulders and a mournful expression may convey that things aren't alright at all.

Convey Information with Regard to the Emotional State

Even if you haven't spoken anything, your facial expression, tone of voice, and body language may sometimes tell people precisely how you feel. Consider how many times you've asked

someone, "Are you OK?" You have a sour expression on your face." We can deduce how people are feeling based on their nonverbal communication.

Cultivate the Relationship Between People

If you've ever observed a couple conversing, you've probably noticed how they tend to mirror each other's body language. They have comparable hand positions, grin simultaneously, and turn to face each other more directly. These actions strengthen their bond by increasing their rapport and making them feel more connected.

Give Feedback to the Other Person

Smiles and nods indicate that you are paying attention and agreeing with whatever they are saying. Your movement and hand gestures may imply that you want to communicate. These subliminal impulses convey information in a gentle yet clear manner.

Manage the Communication Flow

We employ various signs to indicate that we have completed speaking or that we would want to talk. For example, an expressive nod and a strong shutting of the lips suggest that we have nothing else to say. You can indicate that you want to speak by maintaining eye contact with the person heading a meeting and nodding slightly.

Learn the Technique of Non-Verbal Communication

Nonverbal communication can be learned like any other language. This meant that every nod, eye movement, and gesture could be read, revealing a person's true sentiments and intentions. This is, without a doubt, correct.

Interpreting Non-Verbal Communication Is a Bit Complex

Nonverbal communication is not a fixed-meaning language. The context in which it takes place influences and drives it. This encompasses both the location and the people involved and also the culture. When two people are having a social conversation, the head's nod between colleagues in a committee meeting may imply something completely different than when a similar action is used to recognize someone across a crowded room.

Non-Verbal Communication Could Be Conscious and Unconscious

Because we can't see ourselves to understand what we're doing, facial expressions are complicated to regulate. As a result, we may confuse communication by transmitting one message consciously while unintentionally expressing another. Interpersonal communication is made more difficult because it is nearly impossible to analyze a gesture or expression on its own precisely. Nonverbal communication is made up of various terms, movements of hand and eye, postures, and gestures that should be interpreted in conjunction with speech, that is, verbal communication. The good thing is that as we grow older and develop, most of us learn to comprehend nonverbal communication. It's an unavoidable element of connecting with others, and most of us use and interpret it without even realizing it. It may be more challenging to interpret consciously as a result of this. If you stop thinking about it, you'll probably know you have a very good sense of what someone was trying to say. The bad news is that nonverbal communication varies greatly by culture.

4.3 The Importance of Non-verbal Communication

It's critical to remember that nonverbal clues are just as crucial as verbal clues, if not more so in some circumstances. Nonverbal communication has a significant effect on the listener as well as the communication's outcome. Nonverbal communication is frequently used in conjunction with verbal communication to emphasize, repeat, reinforce, refute a verbal message, or replace it entirely. A partner, close friend, or family member may be able to read an individual's nonverbal clues more easily. This nonverbal understanding may allow greater closeness and enhance bonds in close relationships, especially when it compliments what is being spoken by a friend or one partner in a partnership. However, it may be harder for people to hide things from those close to them when something does not feel right, and efforts to do so may lead to misunderstandings or conflict in the relationship. Since nonverbal communication is often unconscious, the way people interact nonverbally may be the first sign of an underlying problem in the relationship that isn't easily visible.

4.4 Types of Non-Verbal Communication

Nonverbal communication comes in various forms and can reveal a lot about a person's thoughts and feelings. Nonverbal communication could be classified to understand its role in daily encounters better. Nonverbal communication comes in a variety of forms. These are:

Body Movements (Kinesics)

Hand gestures, nodding, and shaking the head are examples of Kinesics, which are often the easiest nonverbal communication elements to manage.

Posture

It refers to the way you sit or stand, as well as whether or not your arms are crossed. The position of the body, by itself and with others, is referred to as posture.

Eye Contact

As a result of the amount of eye contact, this aids in establishing the level of trust and trustworthiness; the direction and focus of a person's eyes are defined by eye contact and motions.

Paralanguage

It includes features of the voice that aren't related to speech, like pitch, tone, and speaking pace. The pitch range in the voice that may express something other than the words spoken is known as tone of voice. Sarcasm, for example, can change the meaning of a person's statements completely.

Closeness or Personal Space (Proxemics)

It determines the level of intimacy. The intimacy level usually varies very much by culture.

Facial Expressions

Smiling, frowning, and blinking are examples of actions that are difficult to regulate deliberately. Surprisingly, the broad facial expressions that convey strong emotions such as fear, rage, and delight are universal.

Physiological Changes

When you're nervous, you might sweat or blink more, and your heart rate is likely to rise. Because they are nearly impossible to control consciously, they are a significant measure of mental health.

Nonverbal Communication in Therapy

Because nonverbal communication is so important in navigating social situations and interacting with others and the environment, it's no surprise that nonverbal communication could be a valuable source of insight in therapy. A counselor who is aware of a person's nonverbal expressions and the words genuinely spoken by the person may be better equipped to detect discrepancies between body language and speech. Alternatively, a counselor might learn more from a person's emotions than from their words. These indicators may aid the counselor and the therapist in identifying and access greater emotional difficulties that the person might not have been aware of. Drawing attention to a person's nonverbal forms of communication and pointing out any discrepancies between what is said and what is communicated without words can also assist a person in becoming more aware of how nonverbal communication is employed in human encounters. As the therapist introduces a little bit of traumatic material, somatic experience, a sort of therapy intended to assist and alleviate the effects of trauma, considers the individual in treatment's body language and physical responses. The therapist assesses the individual's reaction by reading nonverbal signs. The therapist examines a client's breath, noises, and movements in body-mind psychotherapy to identify counterproductive behaviors and assist the individual in developing new ones that have a more beneficial impact.

4.6 Cultural Differences in Nonverbal Communication

In different cultures, several types of nonverbal communication have distinct meanings. For example, in the United States, a gesture or action may signify one thing but indicate something quite different in Japan. An American would most likely point with their index finger, whereas a Japanese person would more likely gesture with their hand; pointing with the index finger is considered impolite in Japan. When it comes to nonverbal communication, one key cultural variation is the presentation of emotion: some cultures are more controlled than others and avoid displaying emotion in public or at all. Some cultures may also repress facial emotion, believing that a moving face indicates a lack of emotional control. Another part of nonverbal communication that varies by culture is eye contact. Direct eye contact is often interpreted as a symbol of trustworthiness and interest in a person's remarks in the United States.

On the other hand, a prolonged look may be interpreted by some as a sign of sexual interest and attraction. Eye contact is often avoided in places such as Japan, where direct eye contact is considered rude. On the other hand, the converse is true in Arabic cultures. In Arabic cultures, eye contact is an indication of interest and honesty.

4.7 Tips for Improving Nonverbal Communication

Mindfulness can help people better comprehend their nonverbal communication styles as well as the communication styles of others. Bringing one's attention to the current moment and paying attention to facial expressions and posture might help one become more self-aware and interact more successfully with others. For example, during a conversation, a person might actively consider eye contact, gestures, tone of voice, body movement, and the other person's reaction to these parts of communication. Nonverbal communication is influenced by stress as well. People who are stressed are more likely to misinterpret others and to put forth verbal signals which confuse others. Stress management can help you improve your verbal interactions and relationships. Identifying and understanding another person's nonverbal clues requires maintaining awareness of one's own and others' emotions. People who frequently feel misunderstood or isolated from others may find it beneficial to question a close family member or close friend how they communicate. When nonverbal communication is inconsistent with spoken words, others may be unsure of their intentions and find it difficult to trust what they are saying. An individual could also use nonverbal communication to convey a feeling that others find offensive, such as judgment or aggressiveness. This might not come across in the individual's spoken words, and nonverbal indicators may send a message that the individual is unaware of. As a result, observing others' reactions and establishing lines of communication can reveal methods to better match verbal and nonverbal communication.

Chapter 5
Dynamics of Relationships

Relationships are an important aspect of life. It can be challenging to find the perfect words to describe diverse relationship roles and dynamics, whether it's with acquaintances or lovers, family or friends, people online or in person, or anything in between. We will assist you in choosing the essential words that are necessary to communicate with significant others more correctly and effectively.

5.1 Accepting

Acceptance in the context of partnerships refers to learning to accept the partner(s) for who they are now and as they change over time, including their traits, habits, and needs. Reflect on your potential inclination to judge, change, or become quickly irritated by elements of who they are as well as how they behave as part of the process of truly accepting your partner.

5.2 Active/Passive

The terms "active" and "passive" indicate a power dynamic that is frequently observed in relationships as well as families. In many aspects of a relationship, an active/passive dynamic can be seen. For example:

- Household chores
- Having complex conversations
- Assuming financial responsibilities
- Initiating foreplay or sex.
- Prioritizing health and well-being.

The active person is typically the one who takes the initiative and makes a decision in a scenario. The passive person is someone who is disengaged, unresponsive, apathetic, or overpowered (emotionally or physically).

5.3 Allosexual

This term and category refer to people who are attracted to each other sexually. The use of this phrase helps normalize the experience of being asexual and gives individuals who aren't part of the asexual group a more precise label.

5.4 Asexual

Individuals with an asexual identity or orientation seem to have little sexual attraction to people of any gender. Asexuality is a broad term that encompasses a variety of sexual as well as romantic identities that characterize people who have little or no sexual interest.

5.5 Balanced

A balanced relationship is the one in which both parties give and take in equal and healthy amounts. In a relationship, assessing how much love, affection, energy, and support you give and receiving is an excellent method to determine which areas feel balanced and which areas could require more focus or intention. Each relationship's definition of balance is distinct, and it depends on each person involved feeling respected, valued, and having their needs addressed.

5.6 Close Friends

These expressions refer to a platonic relationship between two friends who share much love, caring, and nonromantic feelings for one another. In terms of care, time spent, and commitment, these partnerships can mimic sexual or romantic partnerships, but they often lack the sexual or romantic component. Admiration, filtration, and commitment are common in platonic friendships between close friends, but they don't reveal anything about either party's sexual or romantic desire or preferences.

5.7 Casual

This refers to a connection that is yet to be defined or branded and needs less commitment than formal or non-casual relationships. Given the ambiguous nature of the term, it's difficult to tell precisely what someone implies when they use it to describe a connection. Casual relationships can have a wide range of meanings and expectations from person to person. Some casual relationships, for example, are sexual, and others are not. It's crucial to discuss how you define a causal relationship with friends and partners so that you're all on the same page and can respect one other's needs and boundaries.

5.8 Changing or Working Hard

These terms allude to the act of directing one's efforts toward changing features of a relationship or an individual participating in one. This "job" is frequently motivated by a desire to improve or enhance the relationship's happiness. While change or hard work in a relationship could indicate commitment, it could also be a sign of incompatibility and that one partner's emotional or physical needs are not being satisfied.

5.9 Civil Union

A civil union, sometimes known as a civil partnership, is a legally binding union between two people. This sort of legally recognized partnership provides only state-level legal protections and privileges. Civil unions have different terms from state to state and do not offer the same federal benefits and protections as marriage.

5.10 Co-dependent

This is a relationship dynamic in which the physical and emotional boundaries required for a healthy and respectful long-term partnership are absent. Though the term "codependent" is frequently applied to people or personal characteristics, it more appropriately describes behaviors, activities, or tendencies. Codependency manifests itself in a variety of ways, but some telltale indicators include:

- You're losing touch with who you are living as a self-sufficient individual
- You don't have your relationships

- Putting the needs of your partner ahead of your own

5.11 Cohabitation

This is the act of sharing a home with someone with whom you are in a relationship. Partners can decide to cohabitate at any point in their relationship for a variety of reasons, including:

- The stage of the relationship
- Convenience
- Personal values
- Financial benefits
- Practicality

Deciding to cohabitate has different values and assumptions for various individuals, so it's crucial to talk freely about what it means in the framework of your relationship (s).

5.12 Committed

This defines a relationship that includes accountability and intention, with particular reference to:

- Time spent
- Ability and intent to work through conflict
- Openness to a future or long-term engagement
- Level of prioritization
- Commitment to meeting one another's needs

5.13 Courtship

This term refers to the time between two people formally entering into a partnership that implies a long-term commitment to a shared future. Culture to culture, person to person, and relationship to relationship, values, and motives attributed to a given courtship can differ.

5.14 Dating

This is the act of engaging in a shared activity to spend time with or learn more about someone. Going on a date, often known as dating, is a common first step in evaluating a romantic, platonic, or sexual connection to someone. Dating expectations differ from one individual to the next and from one culture to the next. In the early stages of getting to know someone you're romantically, platonically, or sexually interested in or attracted to, talking about what dating means to you can help encourage communication, honesty, and trust.

5.15 Disconnected

Disconnectedness alludes to distant feelings as well as a lack of emotional connection in a relationship. One or more of the following factors might lead to emotional disconnection:

- You're not having your needs addressed
- Searching for someone outside the relationship to help meet your specific needs
- A communication breakdown
- Mutual incompatibility

5.16 Dominating

Dominating or domineering is a term that can be used to characterize a person's or a relationship's characteristics. Dominating, sometimes contrasted with "submissive," refers to asserting sexual, physical, financial, emotional, or psychological control in a relationship, scenario, or specific encounter. When a person and relationship dynamic possess dominating characteristics, it can result in a short or long-term power imbalance in the relationship. For some, this power shift is a good thing since it helps with compatibility and attraction. Others may perceive this shift as intimidating, insulting, or nonconsensual. Discussing your observations regarding dominance and dominating tendencies in a relationship could help you and your partners confront power dynamics with honesty and intention and provide you with a better understanding of the role that power plays in your relationship.

5.17 Domestic Partnership

The term "cohabiting relationship" refers to a partnership in which two people live together. They have a romantic connection but are not legally married. Domestic partnerships have the same legal status as civil unions and marriages, but they do not have the same advantages, rights, or advantages.

5.18 Engagement

The time in a relationship before a legal, formal, or ceremonial commitment is referred to as this type of relationship. However, this type of relationship is only viable if both partners agree to this long-term commitment. Some individuals identify engagement with a proposal from one person to another or the gifting of a ring, while others may not link it with any particular action or tradition.

5.19 Friends with Benefits

This term refers to a relationship with components of friendship and another relationship dynamic, most commonly romantic or sexual attraction. Each person involved determines the specific benefits of friendship, which can differ from relationship to relationship. Some people use the term to express their wish to keep things informal or interact with other people. Some use this term to describe a desire for the relationship to be more like a friendship.

5.20 Long distance

This term is used to define relationships between people who don't live in the same town, city, state, or country and don't get to see each other as much as they would have lived in the same town, city, state, or state country

5.21 Marriage

Marriage, in general, refers to a socially recognized and legally binding commitment between two individuals that brings their lives together and offers them specific rights and privileges. It's crucial to remember that the social and legal definitions of marriage vary depending on geographic area, culture, religion, and personal values.

5.22 Monogamous

This is a relationship in which the participants agree to only have one primary mate, sexual partner or romantic interest. This form of partnership is also known as an exclusive relationship. People in dyadic relationships, often known as couples, are most typically described as monogamous. It can also apply to a group of people in an exclusive relationship who have agreed to exclusively have a physical, sexual, or romantic relationship.

5.23 Non-Monogamous

Non-monogamous refers to a partnership that allows for romantic, physical, or sexual involvement or relationships with other people or in several committed relationships.

5.24 Open

This is a colloquial term for a partnership that allows for romantic, physical, emotional, or sexual activities in multiple relationships. Some open blocks are built around a committed primary connection, while others don't value one relationship over other romantic, physical, emotional, or sexual interactions now or in the future.

5.25 Partner

This is a broad term that refers to anyone you are in a relationship with or with whom you have romantic, loving, emotional, or sexual sentiments. Partner is frequently used in conjunction with another term to more precisely describe the type of partner a person is and provide extra information and context about the relation in question. Here are a few examples:

- Romantic partner
- Partner for life
- Parenting partner
- Marriage partner
- Love partner
- Sexual partner

5.26 Platonic

This is a relationship or friendship that is intimate and affectionate but without romantic, physical, emotional, or sexual attraction or interactions.

5.27 Polyamorous

This is a kind of relationship dynamic or relationship in which multiple romantic, emotional, or sexual relationships can exist at the same time.

5.28 Polygamous

Polygamous means the practice of polygamy, as opposed to polyamory, which allows for many partnerships which are self-defined or based on an agreement or parameters, decided entirely by those participating in the relationship. Polygamy is a type of partnership in which one person wishes to have numerous legally and culturally recognized marriages and spouses.

5.29 Rebound

This is the brief period immediately following a change in the dynamics of a relationship or the end of a partnership. When the phrase "rebound" is used to describe a person, it usually refers to someone who has just ended or modified the parameters of a relationship and is the target of that person's affection, love, attention, romantic, as well as physical desire.

5.30 Relationship anarchy

Relationship anarchy, sometimes known as RA, is a term pioneered by queer feminist Andie Nordgren. It's a relationship type or dynamic that only has roles, expectations, rules, and agreements that are consciously supported by the people in the relationship(s). A relationship anarchist's specific language and ideas differ from person to person as well as relationship to relationship, although essential principles like non-monogamy as well as lack of hierarchy are generally shared.

5.31 Significant other

This is a gender-neutral and inclusive way to refer to someone you're dating or in a relationship with. This is a broad phrase that can be used to describe someone in a variety of relationships, including (but not limited to) casual, polyamorous, formal, monogamous, committed, or open ones.

5.32 Sexual partner

This is a broad term for a relationship in which you have sex and have physical intimacy with someone.

5.33 Spouse

This is a gender-neutral term that refers to someone involved in a legal partnership, including a marriage or civil union.

5.34 Temporary or Just for Now

These are everyday phrases for relationships in which one or more of the partners do not intend to commit to a longer-term or future relationship.

5.35 Toxic

- This describes a relationship dynamic that usually has one or more of the following characteristics:
- Damaging
- Destabilizing
- Abusive
- Controlling
- Codependent
- Emotionally draining
- Socially isolating
- Unhealthy
- Unbalanced

5.36 The bottom line

The phrases or terms we use to define relationships evolve, and they can also be influenced by your culture, religious beliefs, and geographic region. Taking the time to learn more about the terms and language people use to discuss relationships can help you communicate more clearly about your relationship status, history, values, as well as the ways you tend to engage with other people—now, in the past, and the future.

Chapter 6
Toxic and Abusive Relationships

Everything works when you are in a happy relationship. Sure, there are setbacks, but you usually make decisions together, discuss any issues freely, and truly enjoy each other's company.

6.1 Toxic Relationships

Toxic relationships are a different thing. When you are in one, it's much more challenging to spot red flags. It could be a clue that things need to change if you routinely feel drained or sad after spending time with the partner. Here are some obvious indications of toxicity in a relationship, as well as what to do if you notice them on your own.

What Does it Look Like?

Toxic signs can range from subtle to overt, based on the nature of the relationship. You may recognize any of these indications in yourself, your spouse, or the relationship itself if you're in a toxic relationship.

Lack of Support

Your time together has ceased to be constructive or supportive of your ambitions.

Healthy relationships are built on a shared desire for the other to succeed in all aspects of life. Then things become toxic, though; every accomplishment becomes a competition. To put it another way, you don't feel like they've your back.

Toxic Communication

Most of your talks are filled with criticism, sarcasm, or overt antagonism, rather than treating each other with kindness. You might even start avoiding each other's company.

Jealousy

While experiencing jealousy is natural from time to time, it could become a problem if you can't seem to think or feel favorably about their achievement.

Controlling behaviors

Controlling behavior, such as constantly questioning where you are or growing enraged when you don't respond to texts right away, can add to toxicity in a relationship. These attempts to exert control over you could be harmful and an indication of abuse in some situations.

Resentment

Holding grudges and allowing them to fester erodes relationships. Frustration or anger can build up over time, widening a gap that was once minor.

Dishonesty

To avoid spending time with your partner, you find yourself making up stories about your whereabouts or who you meet up with regularly.

Signs of disrespect

A red sign includes being consistently late, carelessly "forgetting" events, and other habits that demonstrate a disregard for your time.

Negative Financial behavior

Your partner may make financial decisions without informing you, such as purchasing big-ticket products or withdrawing vast sums of money.

Perpetual Stress

Every relationship has some level of stress, but it's a sign that something isn't suitable if you're continuously on edge. This constant tension can harm your physical and mental health.

Ignoring the Needs

It's a solid sign of toxicity if you go along with whatever the partner wants to do, even if it goes against your wishes or comfort level. You might, for example, consent to a vacation they arranged on dates that aren't convenient for you, either intentionally or unintentionally.

Lost Relationships

To prevent disagreement with your partner or prevent having to explain what's going on in your relationship, you've ceased spending time with relatives and friends. Alternatively, you may discover that your leisure time is consumed by resolving issues with your partner.

Lack of Self-Care

When you are in a toxic relationship, it's easy to neglect your typical self-care routines. You might stop doing things you used to enjoy, disregard your health, and give up your leisure time.

Desiring for change

You may choose to maintain the relationship because you recognize the other person's potential or because you believe that if you alter yourself and your behavior, they will change as well.

Bringing up Issues Could Exacerbate the Situation

You're afraid that bringing up issues would cause many conflicts, so you become conflict-averse and keep your concerns to yourself.

Can the Toxic Relationship be Saved?

Many people believe that toxic relationships are doomed from the start, but this isn't always true.

The desire to change on the part of both parties is the deciding element. If only one partner is committed to developing healthy habits, there is a slim chance that anything will change. Here are a few more indicators that you'll be able to resolve your issues.

Willingness to Invest

You both have an open approach and a willingness to put effort into improving your relationship. This could take the form of a desire to have more in-depth conversations or a desire to set aside regular blocks of time to spend quality time together.

Acceptance of Responsibility

On both ends, it's critical to recognize past acts that have affected the relationship. It demonstrates a desire for self-awareness and accountability.

Switch from Blaming to Understanding

There may be a way forward if you can both redirect the dialogue away from blame and toward understanding and learning.

Openness to Outside Help

This is a significant issue. Individual or couple counseling may be required at times to help you get things back on track.

How Can We Move Forward?

This would take patience, time, and effort to repair a toxic relationship. This is especially true considering that most toxic relationships result from long-standing problems in the current relationship or unresolved issues from previous relationships. Here are some suggestions for getting things back on track.

Don't Live in the Past

Yes, dealing with past occurrences will very certainly be an element of mending the relationship. However, this should not be your relationship's main focus in the future. Refrain from bringing up negative scenarios all of the time.

Your Partner Must Be Viewed with Compassion

When you find yourself needing to blame the partner for all of the difficulties in your relationship, take a step back and consider the possible motivators behind their actions. Have they been having difficulties at work? Was there some familial drama on their minds? These aren't justifications for poor behavior; they can also help you understand where your partner is coming from.

Initiate the Therapy

A positive attitude toward therapy can indicate that harmful issues can be resolved, and relationships can be saved. Following through on this would be crucial in assisting the connection to progress. Individual therapy could be a beneficial addition to couples counseling, which is an excellent beginning point.

Look for Support

Irrespective of whether you choose to go to therapy or not, seek other ways to help. Perhaps talking to a trusted friend and joining a local support group for couples and partners dealing with specific challenges in their relationship, such as adultery or substance abuse. This will be a good place to start.

Practice Constructive and Meaningful Communication

As you fix things, pay special attention to how you talk to each other. Be kind to one another. For the time being, avoid sarcasm and tiny barbs. Focus on using "I" statements, particularly when discussing interpersonal concerns. Instead of expressing, "You don't listen to what I'm saying," say, "I feel like you aren't listening to me when you pull out your phone while I'm talking."

Try to Be Accountable

Both partners must accept responsibility for the toxicity. This entails recognizing and taking responsibility for your behavior in the relationship. Being able to participate fully during uncomfortable conversations is also important.

Heal Individually

It's critical for each of you to figure out what you want out of the relationship and where your boundaries are. Even if you think you already know what the requirements and boundaries are, it's a good idea to go over them again. The process of mending a broken relationship provides an excellent opportunity to reconsider your feelings about specific aspects of the relationship.

Give Time to the Significant Other for Evolving

Keep in mind that nothing happens overnight. As you mature in the following months, try to work together to be more flexible and patient with each other.

Abuse vs. Toxicity

Toxicity in a relationship can manifest itself in a variety of ways, including abuse. Abusive behavior can never be justified. It's improbable that you'll be able to change your partner's conduct on your own. Abuse comes in a variety of forms. This can make it difficult to spot, especially if you've been in a toxic relationship for a long time. The following signs indicate emotional or physical abuse. It's usually wise to leave if you identify any of these in the relationship.

Diminishing Self-Worth

Your partner holds you responsible for everything that goes wrong, making you feel as if you are incapable of doing anything right. You'll feel small, ashamed, and drained as a result. They may do it by patronizing, disregarding, or publicly embarrassing you.

Stress and Continuous Anxiety

It's natural to be frustrated with the partner or have worries about your relationship's future. However, you shouldn't spend too much time thinking about the relationship or your safety and protection.

Risk of Separation from Friends and Family

When you are in a toxic relationship, it's natural to withdraw from family and friends. An abusive partner, on the other hand, may cause you to remove from your support system. To distract you, they might, for example, disconnect the phone while you are talking or get in your face. They might even persuade you that the loved ones don't want to hear from you in the first place.

Interference with School or Work

Isolating and controlling you by prohibiting you from pursuing a job or studying is a strategy for isolating and controlling you. They might also try to embarrass you at work or school by raising a scene as well as talking to your employer or teachers.

Fear and Intimidation

An abusive partner may erupt in wrath or use intimidation methods like pounding their fists against walls or refusing to let you leave the house during a fight.

Name-calling and Put-Downs

Verbal abuse includes insults aimed at humiliating and undermining your interests, attractiveness, or accomplishments. Here are some samples of what a verbally abusive partner might say:

- You have no value
- You're incapable of doing anything correctly
- No one could ever love you as much

Financial Constraints

They may have complete control over all incoming funds, preventing you from opening your bank account, limiting your access to credit cards, or just providing you with a daily stipend.

Gaslighting

Gaslighting is a psychological manipulation method that causes you to doubt your own instincts, feelings, and sanity. They can try to persuade you that they've never been abusive, arguing that it's all in your brain. By appearing like the victim, they may accuse you of having anger and control issues.

Threats of Self-Harm

Manipulation and abuse are when someone threatens you with suicide or self-harm to get you to do something.

Physical Violence

Physical violence can result from threats and verbal abuse. If your partner starts slapping, hitting, or pushing you, it's evident that the relationship has deteriorated.

Chapter 7
Healthy Communication in a Relationship

The key to a happy relationship is effective communication. If you don't make an effort to connect, your relationship may never develop. One of the key building elements of any good, happy, and long-lasting relationship is communicating effectively. Although it's practically impossible to have perfect communication skills all of the time, if you and your spouse work hard to break negative communication patterns and embrace good ones, you should be able to navigate any problematic talk successfully. Here is what you should do to ensure that you're prepared to solve difficulties and express your thoughts in a healthy, productive manner.

7.1 Why Is Communication in Relationships Important?

To have a happy and healthy relationship, both partners must communicate. Because you spend most of your time with your partner, there's a higher chance of misunderstandings and conflict. However, you will be rewarded if you master relationship communication.

Increased Trust

In a relationship, true communication means that you may talk to your partner about anything: your joys and sorrows, your good and terrible days. You're willing to be vulnerable in front of them since you know they'll always love and support you. One of the five disciplines of Love is absolute courage and vulnerability, which leads to entire trust in your partnership.

Skills to Resolve Conflicts in an Amicable Manner

Many couples seem to quarrel constantly—and some who don't seem to quarrel at all. While all partnerships have their ups and downs, frequent fighting and no fighting at all are indicators of a lack of communication in a partnership. It's not necessary to agree with your partner all of the time. It's to use the recommended tactics and methods to develop your conflict resolution abilities so that you can convert them into something that improves your relationship rather than tearing it down when conflicts arise.

Enhanced Intimacy

Learning how to increase relationship communication is beneficial to your emotional closeness or ability to listen, understand, and be sensitive to your partner. Practicing communication skills demonstrates that you appreciate and cherish your partner's feelings and viewpoints. Emotional closeness soars—and physical intimacy grows—when people feel appreciated and accepted in this way.

7.2 Over-Communication in Relationships

In some situations, there is an excess of communication in partnerships. Internalizing and externalizing are two frequent coping techniques used by anxious or unsure persons of how to express themselves. When faced with a conflict, people who internalize prefer to shut down and retreat; those who externalize want to talk it out, often excessively. In both of these cases, MORE communication doesn't necessarily equal GOOD communication. Externalizers may need to slow down and refine their message, whereas internalizers may require more space before they can speak. Instead of saying more, consider how you might say it more effectively.

7.3 How to Communicate in a Relationship

In partnerships, communication can mean the difference between a great, long-lasting relationship and a tumultuous relationship that ends in disappointment. It is critical to improving one's communication skills.

Be Open, Honest, and Vulnerable

When it comes to increasing communication in a relationship, being honest and open is at the top of the list. Make your sentiments and needs to be known by saying exactly what you mean. Retreating from disagreement may appear to be a secure and comfortable place to be, but it is no alternative for trust in a relationship, and it will never help you improve your communication skills. Walking away from an argument is a temporary solution to a persistent communication problem that should only be used for a brief cooling-off time. When you and your spouse disagree, you should be able to trust that whatever you say will be heard and appreciated and that your partner will do the same. If you, as well as your partner (or both of you), are conflict-averse, you may find yourself suppressing your feelings to please each other and prevent difficulties. This interim peacekeeping solution turns a two-way connection into a one-way street, which isn't a long-term solution. The enjoyment and intimacy you used to enjoy will decrease with time, and the relationship will suffer as a result. Instead of disregarding problems, you both must improve your communication skills. Although being vulnerable with someone can be frightening, you won't be able to get to the base of an issue or disagreement if you're unable to be honest and open about your feelings. Healthy communication does not entail lying or distorting one's feelings; rather, it entails being completely honest with one another. In any relationship, healthy communication is predicated on both partners being open and honest with one other. You're on the correct track if you can respect each other and listen to what the other person has to say."

Do Everything Face-to-Face

It's unreasonable to expect all communication in a relationship to take place face to face, mainly if your relationship is based on long-distance, but it's much better to talk in person about the essential stuff than to try to resolve the dispute over the phone or, worse, text. Having critical conversations face-to-face to minimize misinterpretation is one of the most critical aspects of healthy communication. Instead of talking to each other, the goal is to talk to each other. It's a small change that could make a big difference."

Do Not Be Judgmental

Coping with the fear of being judged is one of the most difficult aspects of opening yourself to someone. However, neither partner in a good relationship would make the other feel criticized for expressing their feelings or thoughts. Healthy communication occurs when two are calm, open to hearing a different point of view or viewpoint. Their objective is to identify common ground, a solution, or simply learn more about the other person, all without reacting with judgment or anger to what the other says.

Commit to True Connection

The most common misunderstanding regarding communicating in a relationship is whether the communication is synonymous with talking or conversing. At its most basic level, communication in relationships is about connecting and using your verbal, written, and physical talents to meet your partner's needs. It's not about striking up a conversation. It revolves around listening to your partner's perspective, expressing support, and letting them know you're their biggest supporter.

It's all too easy to lose sight of genuine connection and passion, especially in long-term partnerships. However, admitting that you're not connecting the way you used to is the first step in improving communication in a relationship. Discuss the possibility of rekindling your relationship with your partner and offer a starting point. Don't worry if your partner isn't on board. Relationships are a perfect location where you go to provide rather than receive. Many of these methods can be implemented without your partner's involvement—and you might even inspire them to reciprocate.

Arguments Should be Aimed at Understanding Each Other and Not at Winning

It's tough not to get engaged in the desire to be the one who wins a debate. It isn't about who is right and wrong when it comes to healthy conflict. Instead, it's about both spouses sharing their viewpoints and working together to find a solution. Healthy communication entails conversing with the goal of better understanding your partner. It's not a contest of who's right or who's wrong. Rather than shaming the other, it aims to establish a bridge between them.

You Must Not Make Assumptions

It's easy to believe what the partner is thinking at any particular time, especially if you've been together for an extended period. However, instead of making assumptions about your partner's feelings, it's critical to seek clarity to avoid unwanted miscommunications. Instead of relying on assumptions, healthy communication aims to clarify what the other person intends. So often, we react based on our assumptions about what our spouse is saying. Each individual can ask for clarification, receive an explanation, and afterward move on to another topic when communication is healthy.

Always Try to Be Deliberate and Not Impulsive

It's difficult not to make snap decisions or say things rashly while you're in the midst of a dispute with your partner. On the other hand, good communication is all about being intentional in both what you say and how you say it. We all communicate differently, but the best communicators share one trait: they do not react impulsively. Instead, they take the time (even if it's only a few moments) to think out what they will say, how they will say it, and when they will say it whenever feasible. This little planning could make the difference between a major misunderstanding and a message that is conveyed correctly.

Both Partners Should Validate Each Other's Feelings

There is practically nothing more annoying than feeling like your spouse doesn't care or understand about how you're feeling, which is why it's so important to learn to validate each other's feelings, even if you don't entirely understand and agree with them. The world's genuinely great listeners do more than merely listen. They pay attention, try to comprehend, and validate. The ability and will to know how and when to affirm your partner's emotions is the final stage that leads to a deep and lasting relationship.

Identify Your Communication Styles

Before you start working on enhancing communication in a relationship, keep in mind that not everyone communicates in the same way. Passive, aggressive, passive-aggressive, and forceful are the four main communication styles. Passive communicators hold their feelings to themselves and couldn't seem to say "No" to the partner. Aggressive communicators are loud and intense, yet they often struggle to form genuine connections with others. Passive-aggressive communicators avoid confrontations and deflect real conversation with sarcasm. Assertive communication is the healthiest: assertive people are aware of their emotions and know how to communicate them successfully. The Meta programs, or how we respond to information, are also a part of our communication styles. Some people prefer to converse, while others prefer to touch, yet others are more visual and respond better to gift-giving than an outward expression of emotion. You know how you choose to communicate, but what about the partner? Communication, as well as relationships are not the same for everyone. Recognizing this will help you communicate effectively with your partner. You must be aware of how your partner conveys this information to you, even if they tell you precisely what they require. You'll miss out on the chance to create trust and closeness if there's a misunderstanding, and you'll both be frustrated. Observe how your spouse reacts to various perceptual cues for a day or two if you want to improve your communication skills. Is he or she responsive to seeing as well as watching, hearing and speaking, or touching and doing? If your spouse is more receptive to language, tone, and other aural cues, for example, establishing a lot of eye contact and using mild facial expressions may not be as effective as you believe. You are sending messages, but they're going unnoticed. If you are an

auditory person and a partner is a kinesthetic person, however, realize that simply expressing "I love you" may not be enough. You need to touch the significant other to reinforce your love and remember to do so frequently.

Discover the Six Human Needs

There are six basic needs that all people have, yet each of us prioritizes these needs differently based on our core values. Once you've figured out which conditions are most important to your spouse, you'll be able to communicate with them in a way that meets those requirements. The demand for assurance is the most basic human need. This urge is what motivates us to seek pleasure while avoiding pain, stress, and emotional dangers. Consider the following questions: In our relationship, how secure does my spouse feel? Different things provide us with a sense of security and comfort. Be honest with the partner about what gives them confidence and stability. The need for diversity is the second human need that impacts communication and relationships. If you know how to communicate with your partner, uncertainty isn't necessarily scary. Healthy challenges which allow couples to grow together are necessary for relationships. As you improve your communication skills, you'll discover that variety keeps things exciting and pleasant with your partner. The 3rd human need is significant. We all want to feel unique and valuable. This need necessitates communication because your partner must understand that you uniquely require them—which they fulfill your needs in manners that only they can. How do you show, rather than just tell, your partner how important they are to you? You can show them by touching them with love, providing assistance when they need it, as well as spending quality time with them. Connection and love are the fourth and final essential human needs. Every person requires a sense of belonging. Good communication in relationships can help us feel more alive by letting us know that we are loved, yet the absence of love can hurt us more than anything else. We neglect to communicate love in a natural, tangible way that speaks to our partner's needs far too often when we automatically say "I love you" to resolve a quarrel with our relationships. Reverse the preceding pattern: Every day, show your partner how much you care in a way that speaks to their tastes and requirements. Learning how to increase communication in such a relationship entails figuring out what "language" your partner says best and communicating with them in that manner. The 5th human need is for growth. The human experience is dynamic, and if we don't keep growing, the relationships will become stagnant. We are constantly striving to improve along the various pathways that most interest us, whether emotional, intellectual, spiritual, or otherwise. Your partner wants growth just as much as you do, and as we improve our communication, we will be better able to grow together. When was the last time you encouraged your partner's development in the areas where they are most enthusiastic? How can you continue to give them your complete support? Contribution and giving are the sixth and last human needs. Remember that giving is the key to life. Our source of meaning is contribution. It shapes who we become and validates our legacy. Consider what you now provide for your relationship and how you may improve. Are you giving your spouse your full attention, the benefit of the doubt, and a second chance? When communication is robust in a relationship, both partners can constantly develop new and better methods to contribute to the satisfaction of the other.

Learn the Three Keys to Passion and Intimacy

Polarity is present in the strongest relationships: contrasting male and feminine forces that complement one other. When either person's needs aren't met, that individual will put on a "mask" of the conflicting energy and isolate themselves from their spouse. When the polarity is fully acknowledged in relationships, though, a lovely connection emerges. Each of the masculine and feminine energies has three basic requirements that must be met. Feminine energies want to be noticed, and they want you to notice and appreciate them. They need to be heard and validated to feel understood. They also require a sense of safety, both emotionally and physically. Masculine energies want to praise and celebrate to feel valued. They must not feel micromanaged or controlled but rather liberated. And kids need to be able to open up to you, so express your feelings and affection openly. In a relationship, communication is all about meeting your partner's needs first. When you do that, they'll be more willing to communicate and connect with you, allowing you to build the relationship you both want.

Determine if You Are Meeting Your Partner's Needs

Ask the right questions and then listen carefully to the responses to determine if the partner is getting the needs addressed in your relationship. Consider what the partner says, and if you're not sure what he or she means, ask by restating their point and confirming that you understand. We listen to our spouse frequently, the secret to communicating in a relationship, rather than the actual vocal conversation. The partner may be expressing the exact nature of the problem, but if you're not paying attention, you'll miss it. Refrain from simply waiting for your spouse to finish what they're saying

before starting your "turn." It's not listening; it's waiting to speak. Instead, pay attention to what they're saying to you with a calm and open mind. This would not only assist you in improving your communication skills but will also allow you to connect more deeply with your partner.

Be Present in Your Relationship

Be present in your relationship to improve communication and truly understand what your partner is saying. Set aside some time and focus entirely on communicating with your partner. They must sincerely believe that you are giving them your undivided attention and that they are your top priority. When you're angry and stressed or working on things that take time away from your relationship, it's difficult to listen and be fully present, aware, and mindful. This is a natural part of life, but it's important to remember that it's no excuse for failing to communicate in relationships. Remember that closeness, love, and trust are formed under challenging times, not in easy ones. We would never advance or adapt if we gave up at the first hint of opposition. Take advantage of these opportunities to learn healthy ways to deal with conflict and stress and watch as you and your spouse grow and bloom.

Let Things Go

Allowing a discussion about what's going on right now to escalate into a reiteration of every wrong you and your partner have ever done is a recipe for disaster. In relationships, this is the opposite of loving as well as effective communication. Instead, evaluate the current situation and determine what you can do right now. Remember why you're here and that your goal, the outcome you care about, is to strengthen the relationship, increase intimacy, and improve communication. Let go of the past because there's nothing either of you could do about it right now. It takes more than just saying nice things to improve communication. Be aware of the body language as well. You can say all the loving and supportive things you want to the partner, but if your arms are crossed over your chest and your face is scowled, your partner is unlikely to respond positively. Listening, loving, and supporting your complete being is how to communicate in a relationship. Lean in close to your partner, keeping your face open and relaxed, and gently touching them. Even if you are at odds with them, show them that you love them with all of your words, actions, and expressions.

Break Negative Patterns

You may be aware of what your partner requires and have considered the desired communication style, but there is another factor influencing communication in relationships: how you speak. According to communication experts, pitch, pace, volume, and timbre are the four components of communication. When you disagree with your partner, be aware of these aspects of your voice and make a determined effort to modulate them. An overly high-pitched voice comes across as defensive and immature. Also, ending a sentence with a higher pitch makes it sound like a question; don't do this unless you're genuinely asking a question, or you risk giving your partner the impression that you don't know what you're talking about. Pace simply refers to how quickly you speak. Take a deep breath and slow down, especially if you're arguing with someone. To get the message across, talk calmly and clearly. Pay attention to volume, particularly volume "creep," and avoid competing for attention—competition only gives rise to shouting and misunderstandings. You won't be able to communicate with the partner if you speak louder.

Listen to your partner if he or she is speaking. Timbre describes the emotional quality, attitude, and tone of your voice. Pay close attention to this and be on the lookout for the red flag timbres like sarcasm, which can erode communication and distrust between partners. Break the pattern when things get out of hand: Keep the conversation moving and progressing in the right direction by being playful and using humor in the right way. Injecting humor into the condition could make it feel less dire and lead to excellent results for you and your partner. That's because humor can help you restore perspective and balance, and it's an integral part of healthy relationship communication. It also reduces stress and enhances physical well-being in everyday life.

The most crucial benefit of laughing in this situation is that it reminds you how much you enjoy just being with your partner. It serves as a reminder that you can enjoy the time together even when things are difficult. It's critical to break the pattern of hostility, hurt, and retreat when learning how to communicate in a relationship. Change your tone when you notice yourself raising your voice and also being sarcastic, for example. If you're constantly blaming your partner and using the word "you," switch to "I" and "me," or even "we." It's pointless to blame your partner for all of your relationship's problems. There are two people involved in every relationship, so don't place all of the blame on them. Breaking the pattern is an effective way to reframe the conversation and return it to a point where you can get to the heart of the matter. Communication in relationships is mostly about understanding your partner's needs, your own needs, and how your relationship can make both of you happy.

Start Over

No matter how hard you try to communicate better in your relationship, an argument will inevitably arise. It's critical at this point to recognize the negative patterns and break them before they can become destructive. You may recall the Cold War if you were born before the mid-1980s. It was a watershed moment in world history when two superpowers with opposing ideologies—i.e., differing values—actually confronted in a tense political conflict that could tip into war at any moment. It was a bad relationship, and in the late 1980s, the two leaders met for a series of talks that would forever alter the course of human history. However, the story of how Ronald Reagan, the US president, and Mikhail Gorbachev, the Soviet Union's leader, resolved the conflict did not begin as well as you might expect. Gorbachev and Reagan were caught in the middle of a fiery debate about the merits and drawbacks of capitalism and communism. As with any political discussion, it was going nowhere, and neither leader knew how to communicate with the other more effectively. Years later, a journalist had the opportunity to speak with both Reagan and Gorbachev and asked them, "What was the moment you decided for peace?" Reagan stood and walked away in the middle of the argument, Gorbachev said, only to turn around and exclaim, "Okay, let's try this again." "My name is Ronald!" There's hope for improvement in the relationship if Reagan and Gorbachev could even start over after so much hate. Always keep in mind that you're in this together because both of you contribute to mutual happiness. Problems are obstacles that must be overcome, and while it's tempting to give up, these are the moments that will define the relationship. Listen to the partner, figure out what their most important needs are, and meet them. When you realize that giving is the key to a happy relationship, you'll work hard to figure out how to communicate with the partner in a way that they can comprehend.

7.4 Communicating Clearly in a Relationship

Communication is an essential component of any healthy partnership and is an essential part of all relationships. Every relationship has its ups and downs but having a healthy communication style can help you deal with conflict and build a stronger, more beneficial relationship. We often hear how essential communication is, but we don't always understand what it is or how to use it in our relationships. Communication is defined as the transfer of information from one location to another. Communication allows you to explain what you're going through and what you need in a relationship to someone else. Communication not only aids in meeting your needs, but it also aids in keeping you connected in the relationship. You must communicate with one another. You can't read your partner's mind, irrespective of how well you love and know each other. To avoid any problems that can lead to hurt, resentment, anger, or confusion, we must communicate clearly. A relationship requires two people, and each person has different communication styles and needs. Couples must find a communication style that is appropriate for their relationship. Healthy communication styles take time and effort to develop. It's impossible to have perfect communication all of the time. When communicating with the partner, be as transparent as possible to receive and understand your message. Check to see if you understand what the partner is saying. When speaking with your partner, make an effort to:

- Set aside some time to converse without interruptions or distractions such as phones, computers, or television.
- Consider what you want to say and be specific about what you want to communicate. Make your message clear so that your partner hears it correctly and understands what you mean.
- Discuss what is going on and how it affects you, as well as what you want, need, and feel.
- Use 'I' statements like 'I need,' 'I want,' and 'I feel.'
- Accept accountability for your own emotions
- Pay attention to your partner
- For the time being, put your thoughts aside and try to comprehend their intentions, feelings, needs, and desires (this is called empathy)

- Share positive feelings with the partner, such as what you admire and appreciate about them, as well as how important they are to you.
- Be conscious of your tone of voice when negotiating and remember that you don't have to be right all of the time.
- If the problem you're having isn't critical, try to let it go or agree to disagree.

7.5 Non-Verbal Communication

We could really say a lot without saying anything when we communicate. Our body language, tone of voice, and facial expressions all send a message. These nonverbal means of communication can convey our feelings to the other person. When our feelings don't match our words, our nonverbal communication is often "heard" and accepted. Saying "I love you" to the partner in a plain, bored tone sends two completely different messages. Check to see if your body language matches what you're saying.

7.6 Listening and Communicating

Listening is an essential component of effective communication. A good listener can help their partner open up and be honest with them. The following are some suggestions for effective listening:

- Maintain relaxed eye contact where it is appropriate in the cultural context.
- Exhibit interest and make gestures by leaning in close to the other person.
- Face the other person in a non-defensive, open, reasonably relaxed posture with the arms and legs uncrossed.
- To avoid looking up to or down on the other person, don't sit or stand sideways. Instead, sit or stand on the same level.
- Glancing at papers, fidgeting with a pen, or tapping the feet or fingers are all distracting gestures that need to be avoided.
- Keep in mind that physical barriers, noise, and interruptions will make it difficult to communicate effectively.
- Turn off phones and other communication devices to make sure you're paying attention.
- Allow the other person to speak in an uninterrupted way.

- Show genuine interest and attention by using assertive statements, be aware of your tone, and be prepared to take a break if you are upset about something.
- It might be a good idea to take a deep breath and relax before approaching the problem.
- Request the other person to provide you with feedback on your listening skills.

7.7 Improving Communication in a Relationship

It is possible to learn how to communicate clearly and openly. Some people find it difficult to speak and may require time as well as encouragement to do so. These individuals may be good listeners, or their actions may speak louder than their words. The following methods can assist you in improving your communication:

- Establishing companionship—sharing your partner's experiences, interests, and concerns, as well as expressing affection and appreciation—displaying intimacy.
- Intimacy is more than just a sexual bond. Having moments of feeling close and being attached to the partner creates intimacy. It entails the ability to comfort and be comforted and the ability to be honest and open.
- Identifying one or two important issues you could agree on, including how finances are distributed, a goal you have, or your parenting styles or strategies.

To improve the way you communicate, begin by asking questions as mentioned below:

- What are some of the things that cause you and your partner to disagree? Is it because you're not paying attention to each other?
- What makes you happy and gives you a sense of belonging?
- What disappoints and hurts you the most?
- What topics do you avoid discussing, and what keeps you from doing so?
- What changes would you like to see in your communication with the partner?

If possible, pose these questions to your partner and discuss your answers. Consider and try out new ways of communicating. Check to see if the results help you communicate better. You will have more control over what happens between you if you're more aware of how you communicate. Opening up new lines of communication, while difficult at first, could indeed lead to a more successful relationship.

7.8 Managing Conflicts with Communication

Given below are the tips that would help you to manage conflict with good communication skills:

- Never use the silent treatment.
- Don't make snap decisions. Rather than speculating on motives, gather all the facts.
- Discuss the events that occurred. Don't pass judgment.
- Instead of defeating each other, try to understand each other.
- Instead of using the past tense, speak in the future as well as present tense.
- Concentrate on the main issue and don't get sidetracked by minor issues.
- Discuss issues that have hurt your or your partner's feelings before moving on to problems involving differences of opinion.
- Instead of saying, "You are," say, "I feel."

7.9 Seeking Help for Communication Issues

If you are having trouble improving communication in the relationship, talk to a relationship counselor. Counselors are trained to identify patterns in the couple's communication that are causing problems, work with them to change those patterns, and provide strategies, tips, and a safe space to discuss issues. You might also think about enrolling in a relationship-related course. It is preferable to take action early and speak with someone about the concerns than to wait until things worsen.

Chapter 8
Tips to Foster Open and Honest Communication in Relationships

If you're in a relationship, you've probably experienced some tense moments. It's healthy to have disagreements because fighting is a natural aspect of being a pair. Working toward a stronger, more intimate link is the cornerstone to any lasting relationship. Communication is vital because it builds trust and a sense of belonging. You should freely communicate in a balanced manner to have an honest, open, and vulnerable connection with your partner. These tactics could help you both improve your communication abilities, whether you are just starting a relationship or have been together for years.

8.1 Recognizing Poor Communication

Before you can enhance your communication abilities, you must first determine which areas require improvement. Here are some warning indicators to keep an eye on.

Passive-Aggressive Behavior

Instead of confronting disagreement head-on, passive aggression is a means of expressing suppressed rage. This could take the form of making jokes about the partner often being late or punishing them by giving them the silent treatment when they are late.

- Criticizing the partner if they tend to get late frequently.
- Making snide remarks about their choices.
- Giving them the silent treatment for their acts.

All of these habits allow you to convey your dissatisfaction without having to communicate it verbally. It may feel good now, but it isn't going to help you in the long run.

Trying to Avoid the Conflicts

Avoiding confrontations isn't going to help either. Ignoring problems only gives them time and room to grow into something bigger in the future.

Using Aggressive Speech

When talking to your partner, becoming openly defensive or aggressive is a sign you have entered into a toxic communication style. The following are examples of aggressive speech:

- Raising of voice.
- Blaming or criticizing.
- Controlling attitude.
- Dominating the conversation.

8.2 Tips for Better Communication

If you identify any of the signs mentioned above in the relationship, the following suggestions can encourage more open and honest conversation.

Process the Feelings in the First Phase

Be sure to examine your own feelings on the subject and calm yourself before speaking with the partner about an issue that is bothering you. When we enter a conversation feeling angry, unhappy, or too emotional, the communication becomes excessively heated and difficult to resolve. Before speaking with your companion, go for a little walk or listen to some soothing music. That way, you'll have better emotional control and be able to speak effectively.

Give Due Consideration to the Timing

When it comes to talking with your partner, picking the correct time is crucial. If anything is bothering you, let your spouse know that you'd want to sit down and talk about it. If your spouse is aware that you wish to speak with him or her, it can help de-escalate the issue because they will be less surprised or disturbed by a heated disagreement.

Start Statements with "I"

The way we speak with the partner can make a huge difference. Couples frequently start a discussion by pointing the finger and assigning blame to the other. It's a good idea to start conversations by expressing how you're feeling. You can do this by employing statements that begin with the letter "I." Instead of admonishing your partner for being overly focused on work, you might remark, "I'm hurt when you're always focused on work." "You're constantly focused on work" is less harsh than "You're always focused on work."

Ensure that Both Partners are Being Heard and Listened

Many couples approach talks as if they are contests or disputes to be won. Even if you disagree with your partner's viewpoint, it's critical to pay attention to why they feel the way they do. They should extend the same courtesy to you. When having a debate, don't make it a contest to see who can develop the best idea. Instead, pay attention to what they are saying and try to grasp what they're saying.

Your target Should Be to Resolve the Issue and Establish an Understanding

Remember that the goal of your discussion with the partner is to reach an agreement. Whether you are bringing up old grudges or addressing divergent viewpoints on future goals, both of you should feel satisfied at the end of the chat. Whether it's dividing tasks or making financial decisions, most resolutions need some compromise. This allows individuals to forgive and move on. It can also elicit sentiments of strength and intimacy between partners.

Try Setting Clear Boundaries

Setting clear boundaries might also assist in avoiding misunderstandings. Consider setting some financial restrictions, for example, if money is a problem. Perhaps you decide that any purchase worth more than $500 should be discussed as well as approved by both parties before even being made.

Keep Your Partner Informed of Your Whereabouts

It may seem insignificant but sending a note to inform your partner of your plans can be incredibly beneficial. It shows the partner that you're thinking of them and is considerate of any potential concerns about where you are, in addition to offering useful information. Leave a quick message for your partner if you know you'll be meeting up with a friend after buying groceries.

Remain in Touch with the Partner During the Day

Daily check-ins in the morning, at lunchtime, and even in the evening are also highly suggested. This would entail taking your mood temperature. You need the partner to know if you are upset before you blow up. To tell your partner how your day is going, use a scale of 1 to 10.

8.3 Communication Mistakes that Should Be Avoided

During the communication, there are certain acts that you must avoid whenever possible.

Discussing Past Mistakes

During a heated moment, it's easy to fall into the habit of revisiting the past. Bringing up your partner's mistakes regularly can backfire and make them defensive.

Yelling and Screaming

During an argument, raising your voice or turning to screaming and shouting is an inefficient approach to deal with your anger. Discussions may get more intense in the long run, eroding your partner's self-esteem.

Walking Away

Disengaging from the partner and leaving a problem unsolved is done via stonewalling and walking away in the middle of an argument. It's understandable if you're feeling overwhelmed and need to take a break. Make it clear that you need to step away from the discussion for a moment.

Sarcasm

When you are debating, keep an eye out for inappropriate humor. It's preferable to make a lighthearted joke about yourself than say something nasty about them if you want to break the ice.

Disrespectful Nonverbal Behavior

Body language may convey a lot of information. For example, if you check the phone rather than facing them and making eye contact, the other person may feel insulted.

The Silent Treatment

People frequently use the silent treatment in the mistaken belief that it establishes limits. However, boundaries are best established when communicating directly with a partner; otherwise, they might not even realize they have crossed one. It's preferable to be strong about a boundary than to assume a spouse understands why you're upset and block them out, which may frequently lead to more relationship damage.

The Bottom Line

Effective communication is the basis of any successful relationship, but it isn't always simple. Consider seeing a therapist, either alone or with your spouse, to work through any underlying issues and build some new tools if you're having trouble communicating in your relationship.

The Importance of Healthy Communication in Relationships

Healthy communication is extremely important in relationships, yet it cannot be easy to put into practice. Every connection necessitates some sort of communication. People who care about one another should be able to converse and share their views, ideas, and feelings. There must be continuous live communication in the life of a man and a woman—not exterior, shallow, verbal communication, but deep and spiritual communication. Shared interests and aspirations, not a

common language, bind two souls. This elicits common emotions such as joy and enthusiasm. All of this can only be found in couples whose members have struggled to retain a regular level of connection and communication.

As a result, whenever something goes wrong in a relationship, the first thing to do is assess communication between the partners. The gradual loss of trust, affection, and self-respect is exacerbated by a lack of openness in communication. Sometimes people live together, yet their relationship is in shambles. This is due to a lack of effective communication. Even though a man is physically separated from a woman, he feels a strong bond with her. If a couple wants to keep their relationship alive, they must make time to interact with each other, regardless of how busy they are. If communication isn't constant, a man and a woman will gradually drift apart, alienation will develop, and the relationship will most likely end in a breakup.

As you can see, communication is crucial to maintaining a healthy relationship. A respectful relationship between a male and a female is the ideal relationship. People need to listen to each other, make concessions, and respect and communicate on any topic. Different points of view are common, but it doesn't mean you can't reach an agreement. Any connection is built on the foundation of communication. The success of a relationship determines its quality. When couples express their pleasures, sufferings, and anxieties, they become closer and establish a common understanding. In a relationship, the skill to communicate is vital.

8.5 What to Do If Your Communication Does Not Work

Usually, men and women quarrel because of certain factors. Some of these are:

- One partner refuses to listen to the significant another point of view
- Both partners seem to dislike each other
- One of the partners fails to give due respect to the other
- Both partners struggle to focus on each other's needs and opinions

Don't hold your soul mate responsible for your problems and misfortunes. After all, in a fight, both parties are always to blame. As a result, part of the personal account must be assumed to prevent your relationship from collapsing. It's critical, to be honest when answering the question, "What went wrong on my end?" What role did I play in the breakdown of the relationship? So, how did I manage to save it? You can spend some time alone to answer these and many other questions. After giving it some thought, one of the partners might realize where they went wrong and be ready to initiate looking for a better solution. It is important to remember that a man and a woman's conflict is a problem in their relationship. And it can only be resolved if there are some shared feelings and a shared desire to save the relationship. As a result, you should exert maximum effort and employ all available methods to save your love.

8.6 Rules of Healthy Communication in Relationships

It is essential to sit down as well as calmly discuss everything that has caused problems. Suppose you are unable to communicate normally but still want to learn more about and understand your partner. In that case, you can seek professional help, such as from a psychologist, or try the following healthy communication exercises:

Express Yourself in an Articulate Way

Cite some examples of the subject of the story to your partner so that the words have more meaning.

Keep Calm

Even if you are in the middle of a heated argument, maintain your composure. It will be easier for you to express your thoughts if you can calm down quickly. Take a deep breath, return to a normal state, and begin a productive conversation if you find yourself becoming angry.

Watch Your Body Language

It can set a positive tone in a conversation. Turn to the woman and look her in the eyes during the conversation. Also, crossing your arms indicates that you are rejecting your partner's point of view.

Try to Get Rid of the Bad Habits which Disturb You

Learn to ask questions as well as talk about your feelings. If you don't, your woman might think you're not interested in her. Don't interrupt the soul mate in the middle of a conversation; instead, wait for her to finish her thought. When you are angry, don't start a conversation. Otherwise, your rage will be transferred to the interlocutor right away. Hold the pause, let your body cool down, and only then begin a conversation.

Be Polite

We are not all perfect, and we all have flaws. However, using them to harm or accomplish something is just the worst thing you can do. Take care of any existing relationships you may have. Why should it be destroyed when it should bring joy? Take care of one another, too. It is in your best interests.

Direct the egoism in a positive direction. Take care of your significant other's well-being, health, and comfort. Instead of demanding and taking, learn to give.

Stop Manipulating

Manipulation is a technique for obtaining what you want from others without bearing any of the consequences. But there are limits to everything: not every desire is appropriate, and not every wish can be fulfilled; however, we can negotiate. The earlier you learn to express your desires, the better your chances of getting what you want.

Listen to Your Soul Mate Patiently

If you are having trouble communicating in your relationships, it could be due to your inattention. You might be able to hear the soul mate, but how effective is it? Perhaps you watch TV, chat on the Internet, cook, and so on. Such communication can hardly be described as efficient and effective.

Talk to Each Other as Often as Possible

Another important and fundamental rule of healthy communication for couples is to learn to talk to each other as often as possible. Every day, we recommend that you spend 15-20 minutes communicating with each other. In this case, listen carefully and without being distracted by other things, react to what your partner says (gestures, facial expressions, questions), and ask again if something is misinterpreted. Discuss what matters most to you: yourself, your experiences, relationships, and what is going on between you. When lovers discuss their experiences, however, things usually quickly devolve into mutual accusations as well as clarifications of who is correct and who is incorrect. This is incorrect. The sooner you talk about your concerns, the less complicated it will be. Learn to be brave and be fair and honest with one another.

Do Not Complain

Do not let yourself look for sympathy and pity from the woman, under any

circumstances, no matter how hard it is. No matter how much you intended to do this and fall into warm women's arms and plunge into the ocean of the sincere female warmth—don't do it. This is one of the best healthy communication skills of men. Learn to make decisions for yourself and, when necessary, for both of you. Don't look into the woman's eyes in search of an answer. Find the courage to decide on your own. Take responsibility of yourself. Take risks even if not all solutions are optimal. Only in this way, a man can maintain his freedom and power in a relationship. And let a woman finally be a woman.

Teach Your Partner to Communicate

Some European women find it difficult to communicate with men for some reason, particularly when it comes to emotional communication. Teach the soul mate to listen and let her know how good it feels to be heard, have your words reacted to, be asked questions, and be given options for solving a problem. Explain to your woman that talking to her will help you figure out a way out of the situation and make the best decision possible. Make an effort to set a good example of how to communicate.

Learn to Communicate the Right Way

Communication styles differ between men and women. Don't try to express a never-ending stream of feelings, thoughts, and experiences. Give information in "portions" so that the woman has the opportunity to comprehend and digest what you're saying. Pay attention to your woman's reaction when you're talking to make sure she's still paying attention. If you notice a hazy expression, try repeating important information more clearly and shortly when discussing your feelings or any other intimate issues that may cause your partner stress, try to create a warm mental atmosphere by sitting next to each other and embracing. This will help your woman relax and comprehend the information better.

You Should Have Something Common

What are the benefits of communication in a relationship? Your union is quite strong if you laugh at everyday jokes and have some ridiculous habit. Being oneself in a relationship is the most challenging task for any partner. You are incredibly fortunate if you enjoy your relationship despite its flaws. You have found your true love.

Appreciate Each Other

It is critical for everyone in a relationship to feel valued. Don't be afraid to compliment your partner. When you or the partner feels undervalued, problems can arise. You should both feel loved. So, make an effort to show and remind each other of your love regularly.

Chapter 9
Marriage, Sex and Intimacy in Marital Relationships

When you are in a sexless marriage that you didn't want or intend to be in, it can be frustrating to devastating. Under certain circumstances, marriages could indeed survive without intimacy, and if both partners are willing to work on it, a sexless marriage can be fixed. Marriage and sex therapists offer advice on how to handle a marriage without sex.

9.1 Marriages Need Intimacy to Survive

When you are in a sexless marriage that you didn't want or intend to be in, it can be frustrating to devastating. Under certain circumstances, marriages could indeed survive without Intimacy, and if both partners are willing to work on it, Intimacy is necessary for a marriage to survive. However, there are many

different types of Intimacy. Physical Intimacy can improve a marriage, but it isn't required for everyone or every couple. Physical Intimacy is more significant to some people than others; the issue arises only when the two people in a relationship argue on its importance. Emotional Intimacy, on the contrary, is frequently required for a couple to feel truly connected, honest, and content. Emotional Intimacy is defined as sharing genuine emotions while also feeling safe, comfortable, and warm. Without this emotional Intimacy, most marriages cannot function properly. Physical and emotional Intimacy are frequently linked, so if a marriage lacks emotional Intimacy, it will also lack physical Intimacy. A sexless marriage can be fixed. Marriage and sex therapists offer advice on how to handle a marriage without sex.

9.2 Sexless Marriages Can Survive

Some couples are fine with a sexless marriage. A sexless marriage is not a concern if it isn't a problem for the couple. Even if one or both partners are unhappy with the lack of physical intimacy, it is a problem that can be addressed and improved over time. If you love your partner and care about your relationship, there are ways to approach the lack of sex between you as long as you're both willing to put in the effort to make it better? It's common, if not universal, for a couple to struggle with sex at some point during their relationship. Because of health issues, aging, increased caregiving responsibilities, and other factors that aren't always fixable, a couple may be unable to have sex. Couples can learn to accept the lack of sex in these situations over time because they love the partner and everything about their relationship. They can also enjoy non-intercourse forms of physical intimacy as well as sexual touch that are still seductive, pleasurable, and connective.

9.3 Not All Sexless Marriages Are Successful

For some people, the absence of physical intimacy could indeed outweigh the other positive aspects of a marriage, leading them to end the relationship. It's especially difficult when one partner is dissatisfied with the level of intimacy in their relationship while the other is perfectly content. You can't make someone change or care about something they don't want to care about. If you are unhappy with your marriage's lack of sex, the most important thing to consider is whether the partner is willing to work with you to make the situation better. If they aren't, it's a good indication that it won't work out. It is not hard to fix this type of relationship, but it will be much more difficult. If you want to improve your sex life but your partner is unwilling to help, you will have to ask yourself some hard questions about your relationship's future.

9.4 When Does a Marriage Without Sex Work?

As long as the couple maintains intimacy and closeness, a marriage without sex could indeed work. If both parties express a desire for a sexless relationship, it must be built on a friendship foundation. Outside of physicality, they must be able to experience pleasure and closeness. This entails sharing the joy, expressing affection, which isn't always physical, and genuinely supporting one another on their journey through life.

- A partner becomes ill.
- A partner develops a disability.
- A traumatic event occurs for one or both people.
- Other life transitions are simply changing the relationship.
- Asexuality affects one or both people-although not all asexual people refrain from sexual play.

The cornerstone for relationship success is associated with a strong sense of likability in the relationship and commitment. If one or both partners still have sexual needs, the couple must find ways to ensure that those needs are met. Every couple's situation may be different. Masturbation, cuddling, hiring a sex worker, or participating in erotic play via play parties could all be options.

9.5 What Is the Solution?

Both the husband and the wife in a sexless relationship must first determine whether they want to be in a sexless relationship. If they do, that is fantastic. If not, speaking with a professional is crucial in deciding how to meet your sexual needs. To reintroduce sex into a marriage, follow these steps:

- Making more time for quality time as well as intimate time in the schedules.
- Getting a better understanding of your requirements.
- Developing the ability to communicate your desires.
- Creating a more positive relationship with the body.
- Getting creative in the bedroom together on non-intercourse activities such as kissing and touching.
- Recovering from past trauma.
- Learning to communicate more healthily.
- Taking care of the relationship's other stress factors.

Engaging with a sexuality professional who can guide you through overcoming sexual avoidance in your marriage can be extremely beneficial. Just remember that bringing sex back into the relationship is entirely possible if both you and the partner are ready to work on it together.

Chapter 10
Interpreting Mixed Signals in Different Relationships

According to sex and relationship therapists, mixed signals can appear in a new romantic relationship as well as with an ex. Mixed signals can be identified in a variety of ways. For a healthy and strong relationship, learning to decipher mixed signals is critical.

10.1 Mixed Signals in a New Relationship

Early on in a new relationship, there can be a lot of passion and curiosity, but there can also be a lot of mixed signals. You may not deduce what your partner thinks until you know the ins and outs of their behavior and communication patterns. Experts have identified six mixed signals that a partner may send early in a relationship:

The partner messages you frequently but does not make plans to go out.

Let's say you met someone at a party, and you clicked right away. You exchange numbers and begin texting (sometimes flirtatiously), but they never request you out on a date or back away when you suggest spending quality time together in person. It's understandable if you're perplexed if he tells you he had a good time and just really likes you but doesn't contact you for a week. This pattern could also be seen on dating apps, where it's even harder to tell where someone stands because you've never met them.

The Partners Are Inconsistent as Well as Unavailable

When you spend in-person time with someone but don't hear from them when you aren't physically together, this is another illustration of receiving mixed signals. In this situation, the only reassurance you may have is the limited amount of time you spend together. Aside from that, they are inconsistent in initiating meetups, calling, or texting. This could all leave a person unsure of what the other person truly desires.

The Partners Need an Emotional Association but Don't Pursue It Truly

Some people will give mixed signals about how serious they want a relationship to become. They may make a verbal promise or indicate a desire to delve deeper, but they don't follow through on actually having the deeper conversations as a couple. They refuse to participate when it comes to questions that may require susceptibility or exposure. This may cause the other person to be unsure about the direction of the relationship.

The Partners Are Present when They Deem It Convenient for Them

When a new partner expresses an interest in being in a relationship but only turns up when it is convenient for them, they send mixed signals. They may tell you that they are always available to listen when you really need them, but they avoid you when things are difficult. They could also limit their face time to situations in which they require assistance or wish to be entertained. The other person may feel manipulated and unsupported because of this.

The Partners Stay in the Relationship for a Specified Time and then Change Their Behavior

This mixed signal is a combination of the numerous mixed signals mentioned above, but it can also be a type of breadcrumbing. It happens when someone texts you frequently, talk about their plans with you, shares personal information with you, and asks you to reciprocate. Then [they] change the behavior, ghost you, and avoid you for some time, change their tone, or act guarded for no apparent reason.

The Partners Flirt with Someone Else

This could send mixed signals if someone who takes an interest in you flirts with other people. This may not be true for everyone, as people's tolerance levels for socio-sexuality vary, but the classic monogamous dater will be perplexed if they observe this behavior in a potential partner. You might not know where you stand if you're on a date with your new love of interest and she flirts with the waiter.

Mixed Signals with an Ex-Partner

Ending a relationship could be difficult, and it can be even more complicated if the relationship ends on good terms. Mixed signals can become extremely common and confusing if you choose to stay friends and maintain contact with the ex. Here are some examples of mixed signals you might get from an ex-partner:

Reaching Out on a Regular Basis with No Intention of Reuniting

If you and your ex are constantly texting, calling, or spending time together but assume you don't see a future together, it can send mixed signals. This is not only perplexing, but it could also make it more difficult to truly end the relationship. That is why some experts advise against making contact after a breakup.

Acting as if Moving on is Fine, then Trying to Meddle with New Relationships

When an ex says they are fine with you moving on, they may make remarks, show up on the dates, or otherwise disrupt the new life as well as relationship. They say one thing (that they would not want to be with you), but the actions speak something else entirely (that they don't really want you to be with someone else). This could jeopardize any surviving relationship with their ex, as well as the ex's new relationship.

Failing to Avoid Sexual Relationship Even after the Break-Up

Exes will sometimes give up the emotional aspects of a relationship to keep the physical characteristics under the garb of friends with benefits. While there are healthy ways to approach an FWB relationship, it could be perplexing in the aftermath of a breakup—especially if one partner is still hoping for a long-term relationship.

Maintaining a Connection Only on Social Media

If an ex constantly interacts with you on social media, whether it appreciates an old photo, posts comments on a new one or shares you funny memes, it can be confusing. These actions may give the impression that they want to stay in touch, but they don't text, call, or make plans to meet in person.

10.3 How to Interpret Mixed Signals?

Mixed signals are hard to understand by their very nature. Mixed signals indicate that the other person hasn't made a formal decision to be consistent or committed to you. It would be easier to identify how to move forward in the relationship if you decide that consistency and commitment are what you require. Staying in such a relationship can cause emotional stress. Suppose their actions are affecting your mental, emotional, or physical well-being, as well as your overall sense of peace but also self-worth. In that case, it's time to consider whether staying in the situation is worth it.

10.4 Why Do People Send Mixed Signals?

When someone behaves in this manner, it's generally a sign that they're dealing with some internal conflict. They may desire opposing or contradictory goals, such as complete freedom while also maintaining safety and security. Instead of taking these mixed signals personally, seeing them as a sign of inner conflict could even help you become a little more compassionate toward them. Overall, mixed signals aren't a sign that you need to change; rather, they indicate that the person sending the signals needs to work on themselves. An avoidant attachment style can also result in mixed signals. When a relationship does become intimate, they tend to withdraw because the feelings of proximity make them nervous. In any relationship, communication is crucial. If you are having trouble understanding someone, being open about this could help you both get on the same page and, hopefully, avoid future miscommunication. If you are honest with your partner about these issues and they don't change, it could be a sign that you're not prepared for the very same type of relationship and that you need to set some boundaries.

Chapter 11
Fixing Lack of Communication for Saving Relationships

Everyone defines communication issues differently. Even more difficult is the reality that within a relationship, different couples will define communication issues differently. Whether we realize it or not, we are constantly in contact with one another and continually communicating. Aside from literal words, we communicate unconsciously through non-verbal languages such as body language and facial expressions and the tone of our voice and our actions. Couples who do not learn to communicate consciously will have intimacy, conflict, and relational growth problems. True connection requires you to understand the partner's inner world and for them to understand yours. If you can't communicate in a way that advances your relationship, you'll find that you grow apart over time. It's impossible to ignore a lack of communication in a relationship, especially when you actively believe like you can't communicate with the partner.

11.1 Signs of the Bad Communication in a Relationship

- Choosing the defensive style.
- Criticizing or dismissing one another.
- Putting up a barrier (i.e., giving the cold shoulder).
- Assuming you have a good understanding of what the partner is thinking.
- Passive aggression.
- Arguments that recur in a cyclical pattern and are never resolved.

- Lacking in compromise.
- There are fewer attempts to interact with one another.
- Arguing about "facts" behind a conflict rather than focusing on what each person went through.

11.2 Signs of an Unhealthy Relationship

While we all do unhealthy things at times, we could all learn to love better by identifying unhealthy signs and adopting healthier habits. If you notice unhealthy symptoms in the relationship, it's critical not to ignore them and recognize that they can lead to abuse.

Intensity

When someone expresses powerful feelings and over-the-top behavior, it is referred to as intensity. Things become too intense in such situations, making you feel like someone is rushing the relationship. They seem obsessed with wanting to see you and be in close contact.

Possessiveness

When someone is envious of you to the point of trying to control who you spend your time with and what you do. While jealousy is a natural human emotion, it becomes harmful when it causes someone to manipulate or attack you. This can include getting upset when you text or socialize with people who make them feel threatened, falsely accusing you of flirting as well as cheating, and even stalking you. Over protectiveness or having

extremely strong feelings for someone are often used to justify possessiveness.

Manipulation

When someone tries to control the decisions, actions, or emotions in a relationship, this is known as manipulation. Manipulation can be difficult to detect because it can be subtle or passive aggressive. If someone tries to persuade you to do things you don't want to do, ignores you till they get their way, or tries to influence the feelings, you're being manipulated.

Isolation

When someone isolates you from family, friends, or other people, it is called isolation. This behavior usually begins slowly, with someone asking for more one-on-one time, but can quickly escalate into demands that you do not see certain people. They will frequently ask you to choose between them as well as your friends, insist on spending all of the time with them, or make you doubt your judgment of your friends and family. If you're lonely, you might start to feel like you're reliant on your partner for love, money, or acceptance.

Sabotage

When someone deliberately sabotages your reputation, accomplishments, or success, this is known as sabotage. Sabotage can include preventing you from carrying out important tasks. Talking behind your back, spreading rumors, or threatening to reveal private information about you are all examples of sabotage.

Belittling

When someone does or says things to make you feel bad about yourself, this is known as belittling. This includes calling you names, making derogatory remarks about people you care about or criticizing you. When someone makes fun of you in a way that makes you feel bad, even if it's meant as a joke, it's also demeaning. This can cause you to lose faith in yourself and your abilities over time.

Making You Feel Guilty

When someone makes you feel like you're responsible for their actions or that it's your responsibility to keep them happy, they may make you feel bad for them by blaming you for things that are beyond your control. This can include threats of harming themselves or others if you don't follow their instructions or stay with them. They may also try to persuade you to do something you don't want to do by claiming that it's significant to them or that if you don't, you'll hurt their feelings.

Volatility

Volatility is when you are scared, confused, or intimidated by someone's extremely strong, unpredictable reaction. When you're around a volatile person, you feel like you have to walk on eggshells, or they'll react violently to the smallest of things. It's possible that the relationship with them feels like a rollercoaster ride with extreme ups and downs. They may have significant mood swings, overreact to minor events, or lose control by becoming violent, yelling, or threatening you.

Deflecting Responsibility

When someone makes excuses for their harmful behavior regularly, they might blame you or others for their actions. Making excuses based on alcohol and drug use, mental health issues, or previous experiences is expected.

Betrayal

When someone is unfaithful or acts dishonestly on purpose, they might act differently around other people or reveal personal information about you to others. This also includes lying, leaving you out on purpose, being deceitful, or cheating on you.

11.3 Effects of Lack of Communication in the Relationship

- Escalated conflict
- Finding it hard to set and reach goals
- Negative perspective of the partner
- Loneliness
- Feeling unseen or unknown
- Lack of intimacy

11.4 Fixing Communication Problems in Relationships

Listed below are the tips for resolving communication issues in relationships:

Identify the Personal and the Partner's Attachment Styles

According to attachment theory, each person's relationship style is influenced by the type of care they garnered from the earliest caregivers. Suppose one or both people in the relationship have an insecure attachment style, meaning they form insecure attachments with others rather than stable and secure ones. In that case, communication will be powered by anxiety rather than authenticity. When a person responds to their own needs for connection by either hopelessly avoiding them (avoidant attachment) or hopelessly pursuing them (secure attachment), they are said to be insecure (anxious attachment). In either case, it's critical to learn about what makes it feel safe enough to participate in genuine communication rather than relying on self-protective measures. If you're dating someone who has an avoidant personality, they'll need a lot of space. You can respond by asking them to communicate in small chunks, giving them time to think, or offering to text or email some of the conversations. If you have a partner who has an anxious personality, it's critical to communicate with them in a predictable and actively reassuring manner.

Explore the Meta-Emotion Mismatch

A meta-emotion mismatch occurs when two people have opposing views on emotions. One partner thinks it's beneficial to talk about and feel feelings, while others believe it's counterproductive. It cannot be easy to communicate when a couple's meta-emotions are out of sync. It's critical to explore what you and your partner think about emotions to get the partner to communicate with you. When you were a kid, how did you deal with them? Were you able to find it helpful? Then you will want to work together to figure out how to communicate more effectively while keeping these facts straight. This could entail learning to let your partner experience the feelings before offering solutions or being more willing to focus on solutions and compromise rather than feelings in specific conversations.

Address Past Hurts Which Haven't Been Resolved

Another possible explanation you might be having trouble communicating is that you haven't fully resolved a painful event in your relationship. Maybe there was a betrayal, or maybe someone said something that was never corrected properly. You will need to handle these hurts, reestablish trust, and also be willing to forgive each other to move forward and start communicating better. If the partner isn't sharing with you, it's a good idea to figure out why— is it a childhood issue? Are they offended by you? Do they simply have a different understanding of what communication entails? Try to bring up these issues with them and figure out what you both require in open and honest communication. You'll almost certainly come up with different answers.

11.5 Communication Patterns That Hurt Relationships and Solutions

We don't know how to communicate with our partners. We must learn to communicate in an intimate relationship. To build healthy relationships, it's critical to recognize, articulate, and respond to feelings effectively. 10

communication patterns can negatively impact our interpersonal intelligence as well as emotional intimacy in a relationship. IPIQ is a measure of a person's ability to hear, understand, communicate, and fully interact with another person. It extends the concept of emotional intelligence (EQ), a phrase coined by Daniel Goldman to include the ability to translate feelings, thoughts, and intentions into meaningful connections with others. In his 1983 book Frames of Mind: The Theory of Multiple Intelligences, Howard Gardner proposed an eight-criterion intelligence model. One of them was interpersonal intelligence. Interpersonal intelligence was defined as the ability to comprehend, motivate, lead, collaborate with, and understand others. Because it extends beyond EQ into the interpersonal realm, developing IPIQ is critical for optimal living. That connection is made possible by communication. Words have the power to harm or heal. They have the power to promote or demote you. They can push you away or pull you in. They have the power to either bring you down or lift you. This is true in any type of relationship: community, collegial, familial, friendship, romantic, and so on. For committed relationships to succeed, IPIQ must be developed. Love is derived from the Sanskrit word *lubhyati*, which means desire. Humans are wired to want to love and be loved. Romantic relationships are just one type of significant relationship that we have in our lives. Like hunger and sex, the desire to fall in love is an innate biological drive. We often act out most of our attachment and loss

experiences or unresolved issues on the intimacy front. So much can be triggered, and even more, can be healed within this field. There are 10 perceptual communication patterns, also known as "love breakers," that stifle, separate, and destroy intimacy.

On the other hand, there are 10 love-making prescriptions to improve your IPIQ and your relationship's quality. Consider the love-breaking patterns which have been active in your relationship. Then, to transform the sabotaging patterns into a deeper sense of connection, consider using the love-making language recommendations. We strongly suggest that you read these with your partner.

The Blame Game

Disdain, defensiveness, lack of trust, withholding, ghosting, and a loss of intimacy result from a love-breaking language such as you always, you never, you are crazy, and so on.

Love-making prescription

Start doing the following:

Fix the problem, not the blame

Replace blame with the benefit of the doubt

Social judgment neural pathway circuits are suppressed in new love, according to studies. You probably don't remember being blamed or blamed while you were in love. Make a conscious effort to give the partner the benefit of the doubt, refrain from making snap decisions, and avoid taking things personally.

Try mindful reflection

When you are blaming the partner for something, take a breath and think to yourself, "How big do I want to make this?" The majority of our worries in life are either illusions or insignificant. There are appropriate ways to communicate without bad-mouthing each other if you consider it important.

Try putting yourself in your partner's shoes

Refocusing the attention on what you are accountable for, and controlling is one of the most significant coping strategies. When you are pointing your finger at the partner, try bringing it back to yourself, not to punish yourself, but to regain self-control, composure, and insight. You might notice that you are having trouble with the shadow effect. You will discover that what you're blaming the partner for is something you're harshly judging yourself for and trying to avoid. What irritates us and makes us react is frequently something we don't want to see or can't tolerate in ourselves.

Employ the power of apology

When it comes to relationship acrimony, the truth is usually somewhere in the midst. The ability to take responsibility goes a long way toward acceptance, forgiveness, and healing. Instead of waiting for the partner to apologize, take the initiative and say, "I'm so sorry for my part." Stay in your lane and let go of the expectation that the partner will apologize next, even if you hope for mutual reflection and ownership. It's great if it comes, which it usually does. If not, at the very least, you will be able to stand firm, in peace, and with a clear mind.

Ask rather than assuming

Misunderstandings and incorrect assumptions are at the root of most conflicts. During one couple's session, a woman expressed her dissatisfaction with her boyfriend's lack of communication while he was on business, and she assumed, "If I were valuable enough to you, you would indeed call more often." Try pausing and expressing something like "I'd like to get clarity" or "I'd like to check in and clear something up together" the next time you find yourself rushing to judgment.

Use the AMOR method

People are usually afraid of being confronted if they speak their minds. Being confrontational has a negative connotation, as does the notion that expressing feelings or requests directly will only result in more judgment, conflict, rejection, or abandonment. Resolving the issue usually necessitates difficult conversations. When confronted with something that deserves to be acknowledged, this method is useful. It also leads to greater intimacy, understanding, and greater humility, empathy, compassion, forgiveness, and growth.

Affirm

Begin with a positive statement, such as "I recognize you love me and would not want to see me sad, which I greatly appreciate."

Message

Share what may be challenging and hard to say and hear.

Overcome

Try to circumvent this pattern so that you could feel even closer.

Resolution

This process will help the partner listen without feeling blamed or threatened and set you both up for better outcomes in understanding and connecting when you can express feelings that were previously difficult to express or communicate an intimidating request for a behavior change.

The Scoreboard Playing Field

I helped you in this matter; what have you accomplished for me recently?" are examples of love-breaking language. Or "You never" creates a skewed field of losers and winners, as well as resentment and competition.

Love-making prescription

Start doing the following:

We are both givers

Relationships in which a clear or assumed giver-taker dynamic exists rarely flourish. When both of you concentrate on being a giver, no one feels cheated or exploited. Instead, they are filled with deep gratitude for one another and greater joy in the act of giving as well as receiving. This will help you re-establish a higher frequency of romance and sex appeal in your relationship and deeper intimacy.

Be more giving

Instead of focusing on who is receiving or giving more, consider, "What would love to do?" This inquiry has a magical quality to it. Listen, share your thoughts, and wait to see what happens.

Ask that "What can I do for you?"

It will produce rather more magical results.

Express gratitude

"I am grateful to you for checking in with me so quickly," says the speaker. "It's always nice to hear something sweet from you." "Have I recently told you how unique you are and how unique you are to me?"

Maker requests and do not demand

Isn't it amazing how two different ways of delivering the same message can result in completely different outcomes? It will give the partnership an endorphin boost and bring back feelings of deep appreciation.

The cause of frustration and distraction

You say things like "We never do anything!" or "Why can't you ever come with me?" Boredom, frustration, inertia, indifference, distraction, as well as decreased desire are the results.

Love-Making Prescription

Start doing the following:

Keep It Fluid, Keep It Flowing

It's easy to become insulated and isolated in today's fast-paced world. Remembering that there is a big world outside of the small radius in which most of us live. Moreover, this world is part of expanding your lens and experience with your partner. Acknowledge yourselves as global citizens and commit as a group to connecting more with your local and international communities.

Use the language

- I will love your company.
- I have got a surprise for you.

- Let us go to a new place we have never visited before.
- Let us both volunteer for this event?

It leads to wonderful discoveries to replace the mundane, as well as newfound curiosity, anticipatory excitement, increased laughter, fun, and connection, and a nourished as well as revitalized relationship.

The Domineering Attitude

Love-Breaking Language looks like this:

- I want to get this
- We must do that
- You are wrong

This kind of language results in the loss of self, resentful, and disconnected.

Love-Making Prescription
Start doing the following:

Move from "I"-centered to "we"-focused
Let go of your fixed mindset and embrace one of growth. You make compromises until both parties are happy. Partnering necessitates integration and, more often than not, concessions. Satisfaction does not always imply that one or both parties have gotten what they wanted.

Be cheerful and helping
"You deserve happiness, and I deserve happiness," you must work on, and who can argue with that? You must be a couple who deeply loves, respects, and admires each other. We have chosen to grow as individuals and as a group and share a wonderful life. It creates a sense of belonging, balance, and well-being.

Scar Tissue

Love-Breaking Language takes the form of:

- You cannot stop doing this.
- You are again on the same issue.
- You always avoid apologizing for your mistakes.

It results in permanent injury due to an emphasis on past cumulative disappointments, hurts, and resentments, an avoidant attachment, communication style, and suppressing the truth of one's feelings, experiences, and desires.

Love-Making Prescription

Start doing the following:

Stay present

In relationships, overreactions are frequently projections of past trauma onto the present moment and our current partner. These projections can come from your childhood, previous relationships, or a previous stage of your current relationship. You could choose to adopt a beginner's mindset once you've realized how this can derail your relationship. You could even relate to each other with curiosity as well as inquiry if you have this mindset. It leads to greater clarity, curing projections of old patterns from childhood or previous relationships, and more joy in the present moment.

The Roommate Rut

Love-Breaking Language is:

- Whatever
- I'm sorry, again
- I forgot
- I don't care

It results in a passive as well as disconnected life.

Love-Making Prescription

Start doing the following:

Be more cognizant of the circumstances

Many of us go through life sleepwalking, and this includes becoming desensitized to our relationships, making it difficult to see and hear the person we chose. The reset here is not an imposition but rather an invitation to reconnect with what first drew you together, to break free from everyday routines, and to share more of yourself. It leads to increased sensuality as well as sexual intimacy, as well as a renewed focus on fun and a reprioritized relationship.

Sameness Is Closeness

Love-Breaking Language would usually be:

- You concur with me, right
- I find it hard to believe that you don't want to do this

It leads to inauthentic attachments as well as a lack of long-term intimacy and connection.

Love-Making Prescription

Start doing the following:

Be who you are

While it's nice to hear what you want to hear at times, people essentially want authenticity in their relationships. This necessitates you being your own person rather than a people pleaser. Pleasers abandon themselves, only to be abandoned by others who have never known the truth about who they are. When you are reasonable to yourself, you will never get lost, which is the most desirable quality to your partner.

Accept and enjoy the differences

Many presumptions, including the idea that opposites attract, contain some truth. You don't need to go after your carbon

copy because you have already been taken, thankfully. Gary Chapman's book *The 5 Love Languages* delves into an important aspect of receiving and giving love. It's critical to share what's important to you and fully comprehend what's important to your partner to have a healthy relationship. These differences can enhance your individual and collective growth, intensifying your attraction to each other if you are committed to staying growing together, love each other deeply, and have more than enough shared vision and common ground.

Remember that you are both evolving beings

We are not sluggish or stuck in time, even if we once shared a viewpoint or a dream in common. If we want to be alive and aware, our inner lives are continually expanding. You and your partner both deserve to make room for this change and growth. It leads to an increase in appreciation, sensitivity, acceptance, respect, as well as intimacy.

The "You Complete Me" Mentality

Avoid love-breaking language such as:

- No one could ever love you like me
- I would not be able to grow and survive without you

It leads to entangled codependency, a loss of self, and the possibility of falling from grace.

Love-Making Prescription
Start doing the following:

Have healthy reliance instead
You have to identify the delicate line between enjoying the partner's companionship and leaning on them for support. You have to stay away from dependency. As a result of this, you could eventually enhance your relationship with your significant other.

Identify your combined goal as larger than the sum of two parts
A linear relationship between two people can feel stale, uninteresting, and suffocating. The triangle symbol is used in both Kabbalistic and Christian traditions to connect a variety of entities, including the divine feminine, divine masculine, and gateway to the divine source of all living things. The Buddhist triangle represents the invocation of love, and many other traditions use this sacred geometry's symbolism. Imagine yourself on a solid foundation on one of the triangle's bottom corners, with your partner on the other.

Lack versus Lust

Love-Breaking Language could be:

- You better wear some makeup before we go out
- Time to join the gum
- Why haven't you gained a raise in salary?
- I wish you could

It results in killing joy, faith, and passion.

Love-Making Prescription
Start doing the following:

Focus on what is versus what is not
This transformation is both uplifting and therapeutic for our minds and hearts. When you first fell in love, you probably noticed and fed the other's well of beauty, brilliance, and promise. You congratulated one another.

Love means doing kind acts
Make a list of what drew you to your companion-be their personality, physical appearance, behavior, lifestyle, or the chemistry between you, etc. Make a conscious effort to share some of it every day. This can be expressed in a variety of ways, including verbal expressions, love notes, acts of service, physical affection, and anything else that would make them smile. Focus on the positive

instead of the negative, and without expecting anything from the partner. You are entitled to freely express the truth of your heart, regardless of whether it is returned. Reset the previous pattern with patience and remember to acknowledge yourself in the same way.

Initiate a respectful process for positive changes in behavior upon request from the partner

When something is missing that needs to be addressed, a courteous and helpful delivery style will become the key to achieving a favorable solution.

It leads to a resurgence of lust.

Exit Threats

Given below are the examples of love-breaking language:

- I'm divorcing you if you do it one more time.
- I'm finished, so just leave.

Uncertainty, worry, insecurity, animosity, and interpersonal instability are the consequences.

Love-Making Prescription
Start doing the following:

Engage the partner
Redirecting your prior patterns necessitates actively reaffirming your commitment. People are afraid of rejection and loss, which prevents them from connecting and getting engaged.

Seek help from a professional
Before you split up, think about investing in professional help. Staying together, co-parenting, or parting ways amicably will benefit you in the short and long term. It leads to a renewed desire to address issues, a sense of security, and the emergence of growth potential.

Ways to recover from mistakes in the relationship
We all make errors. Many people have a hard time admitting their mistakes, big and little. Requesting a redo is a method to show more respect for others while also bolstering your credibility. There are some blunders that you will never be able to undo. In most circumstances, requesting a second chance can be a practical approach to demonstrating good intentions. Of course, asking can be the most difficult part. Here are some examples of how to use the do-over approach.

Change your habits

Habits are the basis of long-term partnerships. You would be the one to recognize that you have a lot of bad habits. It's difficult to break old habits. It would go a long way to indicate that you are trying if you can say to your partner, "Let me try that again."

Stop apologizing

Men and women have difficulty apologizing to their partners, but a do-over can replace an apology for some of the mistakes we all commit daily. Instead of feeling like you're being forced to eat crow when an apology is required, consider it a good opportunity to express your affection. This makes uttering, "Let's try it again," a profoundly personal gesture, a starting point for mending and, occasionally, romance.

Display intent

Saying "I'm sorry" is crucial for severe wrongdoings, but it's typically only the beginning. If your error is morally reprehensible—say, telling a lie that impacts your entire family or violating a significant vow—the preparation as well as execution of the do-over will reveal your true intentions.

Try to return good acts of the partner

Can you offer someone a second chance even if they don't ask for it? You may either become angry and hold a grudge or let it go when it comes to common mistakes like neglecting to pick up the dry cleaning, screaming unnecessarily once in a while, or being constantly late for date night. Consider the relationship as a savings account for your emotions. Your balance will be high if your partner is generally supportive and affectionate, and you can afford to offer the significant other a penalty-free withdrawal now and then.

Ask for help

We may require assistance with all areas of the do-over, from admitting

responsibility to devising a strategy to correct the error. Here are some indicators that professional help is needed:

The apologies do not appear to be genuine. There can't be a do-over unless there's a desire to change or believe that change would occur.

Negative encounters, like put-downs or criticism, continue to occur. Even with the greatest of intentions, old communication habits can be tough to break.

There is no consensus on a course of action. Both parties must be on the same page regarding how to make the do-over a reality.

Chapter 12
Effective Communication Skills for Healthy Marriages

ommunication is the foundation of a happy marriage. It refers to how you and your spouse interact, share ideas, and resolve conflicts. Relationship communication abilities are difficult to come by. Some couples may have to work on their skills for years. They will, however, be able to interact with one another honestly and openly over time. Irrespective of how close you and your partner are currently, there is always an opportunity to deepen and enhance your relationship.

12.1 Give the Partner Full Attention

Don't text and talk at the same time. You should give your spouse your undivided attention whether he or she is telling you a joke as well as disclosing a deep family secret. Remove all distractions, mute or switch off the television, as well as lean in

close to your partner. This will demonstrate that you value their personal information. Nodding and maintaining eye contact are both effective ways to prove that you are paying attention to your partner. To reduce technological distractions, designate a space in your home where electronics can be kept.

12.2 Do not Interrupt the Partner

The easiest way to intensify an argument is to be interrupted. It's critical that both you and your partner feel like they have an opportunity to speak and be heard when communicating. While it may be tempting to jump in with your own opinion even when your partner is still speaking, especially if you believe they are incorrect on a fact, it is critical to wait. Giving your partner your undivided attention while remaining focused and connected demonstrates your respect for them.

12.3 Create a Neutral Space

It's not always easy to communicate. Many couples find that discussing "tough" marital issues at a neutral location, like the kitchen table, is beneficial. It may seem silly but debating the partner's lack of sex prowess in bed could make them feel unwanted and cause them to have negative feelings about the bedroom in the future. Another illustration of a partner feeling like they have the proverbial "high ground" in an argument is arguing at a relative's house.

12.4 Be Honest with the Spouse

Being truthful isn't always easy, but it's essential for a happy relationship. Honesty, good communication, and trust were listed as some of the highest qualities in a study about "12 Healthy Dating Relationship Qualities." Being truthful entails informing the partner when you believe there are major problems that need to be addressed. It also entails admitting when you've made a mistake and apologizing rather than making excuses. Honesty fosters genuine open communication between you and the spouse and aids in the development of trust.

How Dishonesty Drains You

Have you ever made up a story to entertain or spare a friend's feelings? Do you know anyone who has admitted to you that he or she lied about how many hours they worked to pad a paycheck? When compared to full-scale corporate fraud, some may consider these "white lies," or minor instances of dishonesty, to be relatively harmless a minor ethical lapse. When it comes to protecting a significant relationship, we might well consider a white lie to be mainly harmless. Researchers have looked into the financial and legal ramifications of small acts of dishonesty like padding expense reports and stealing pens. Small acts of dishonesty have unexpected consequences for emotional intelligence, affecting our ability to read the emotions of others. According to the research, the harm is actual and long-lasting. According to a series of studies, deception can impair a person's ability to communicate with peers, even those not involved in the original lie. According to the study, people who engage in dishonest behavior are far less likely to see themselves as relational (for instance, as a sister, colleague, friend, or father) and thus are less accurate in judging the emotions of other people. Because work relationships could be either generative—a basis of enrichment and vitality or corrosive, which is a source of dysfunction and pain—this research is essential to understanding the underpinning interpersonal dynamics in organizations. The ability to accurately read and respond to others' emotional states facilitates supportive, pro-social, and compassionate behaviors, which is especially important in professional settings when building strong networks. Those who are deceitful at work might well experience a negative spiral of mutual misunderstandings as well as missed opportunities for building supportive relationships, which could be detrimental to individuals as well as the organizations in which they work, due to an increase in relational distance as well as a decrease in empathetic accuracy. According to research, subjects who lied were less accurate in judging their partner's emotions than those who told the truth. Those in the dishonest group were not exposed to tell big lies; instead, they were told to make up a story about job hunting that would excite others and make them feel better about their own recruiting experiences. The other half of the participants in the study were asked to tell a story about their real-life job search experiences. The study also discovered that participants who were asked to lie were significantly less accurate at detecting their partner's emotional state than those who told the truth. Surprisingly, these small acts of dishonesty with no malice clouded a person's ability to understand emotions in future interactions. Those people who were tempted and likely lied to each other performed worse on the empathetic accuracy test as compared to those who did not have the opportunity to be dishonest in any of the four experimental studies with a total of 1,879 participants. The effect was also found to be driven by a decrease in how dishonest relational participants viewed themselves. Dishonest people were less likely than those who were honest to characterize themselves in terms of relationships. Subjects who were dishonest disassociated themselves from others, resulting in a decreased ability to read others' emotions. The study also discovered that the more often employees engaged in unethical behavior at work, the lower their empathetic accuracy score, implying a negative relationship between the two. There was one characteristic that protected people from the harmful effects of dishonesty. Those with a naturally high level of social sensitivity and attunement to fragile social-emotional cues in the environment did not show a substantial reduction in the empathetic abilities regarding moments of dishonesty, according to a lab study of 100 adults. However, the average participant in our studies showed a negative effect. Importantly, it was discovered that dishonesty could have downstream consequences: participants who cheated for financial gain were more highly likely to dehumanize the actors in these videos blatantly. This means that they rated the actors as less human than those who did not have the opportunity to cheat. Cheaters were also more likely to engage in deviant behavior regularly. This finding suggests that we may distance ourselves from others when we engage in dishonesty by treating them as being less than humans. This continues down a path of unethical behavior in the future. The findings suggest that even minor acts of dishonesty could have far consequences, potentially jeopardizing a fundamental tenet of our humanity.

12.5 Talk About the Little Things

When you and the partner could really talk about the little things and also the big things, it's one of the best communication skills you can have in a relationship. Talking

about the day, your thoughts, or sharing funny stories from your week can strengthen your marriage. Every topic ought to be open for discussion when you're married. There should be nothing too embarrassing as well as uncomfortable to share. You'll find it easier to talk about more important issues in the future if you start with the small stuff.

12.6 Use the 24-Hour-Rule

There are bound to be stumbling blocks when two people marry and live together. When your partner is nearby, you may feel as if rainbows and butterflies float through the home. When your spouse is nearby, you may feel a headache coming on. If you're angry with the partner and about to say something, take a breath and think about it. Follow the 24-hour rule. As a result, she failed to empty the dishwasher, and he was unable to pick up his socks. Is this the end of the world as we know it? Will it make a difference in 24 hours? If it isn't, think about letting it go.

Make Physical Contact

Physical contact is very important regardless of the tone of your conversation. Low-intensity skin stimulation, such as touching or stroking a partner's arm, stimulates the release of oxytocin. The love hormone encourages romantic partner's relationship and helps them empathize with one another and act as a stress reliever and encourage cooperative behavior.

Make Communication Fun

Communication refers to how you and your spouse discuss family and financial matters, problems and solutions, and how you make decisions together. But don't forget that communication should be enjoyable as well. When you talk

with your partner, you usually share funny stories, future dreams, and deep conversations. These are the moments that foster a stronger emotional bond and increase dopamine levels. Whether the dialogue which follows is serious or silly, make sure to check in with the spouse verbally.

Conclusion

The key to a healthy and happy relationship is communication. You can improve your marriage communication by being honest and open about your physical and emotional needs, keeping your finances open, and giving your partner your undivided attention.

Chapter 13
Communication Tips for A Happy Relationship

You must have figured it by now that communication is the key to any relationship. It may sound corny, but it's true. It's easy to tell people that communication is the key to a healthy relationship but explaining how to communicate is more complicated. We will never be able to open the door to good communication if we're never taught how to use this key. The successful transmission, as well as sharing of thoughts and feelings, is referred to as communication. Communication entails healthily expressing yourself, listening to your partner when they do the same, and truly hearing and absorbing what the other person has to say. Communication is, after all, a skill, so there's always room to improve. Work with the partner to figure out how to stay on the same page and maintain healthy communication. Be as forthright, direct, kind, and considerate as possible.

13.1 Simple Tips for Keeping Your Relationship Strong and Healthy

It's no secret that a strong and healthy marriage requires more than love. Strong feelings for each other are necessary but finding quality time with the significant other can be difficult with all of life's responsibilities. Fortunately, there are many ways to provide your relationship with the love and compassion it requires to thrive. Best of all, many of them don't necessitate a significant change in the daily routine or a significant financial investment. Here are some easy ways to maintain a solid and healthy relationship.

Greet Each Other When You Come Home

First and foremost, say "hello." It may sound corny but making sure you greet the spouse when they return home is crucial. It expresses your delight at seeing your lover and frequently translates to "I've missed you." Let's face it, it's discouraging when you come to an event and that no one welcomes you or seems to notice that you've arrived. When your spouse returns home, remember to include them with a warm "hello" and a nice kiss. Even a few minutes spent completing some daily activities can make a massive difference in the quality of your relationship.

Spare Weekly Time for Your Family

Carrying your kids from doctor's visits to practices to school as well as back to home seems to go on forever. We live in an era of perpetual "go, go, go," which is why weekly check-ins with the spouse are essential. A weekly gathering may not appear to be the most romantic of activities. However, when the kids have gone to bed, pour yourself a glass of wine or meet for coffee during the lunch break. There are numerous ways to spend thirty minutes every week simply by checking in. This is an opportunity for you to reflect on the previous week's events or set plans for the coming week.

Do not Forget to Date the Spouse

Isn't it true that just because you are married, you find it difficult to date? You must be dating because you are married, not because you are single. It's easy to become trapped in the hamster cycle of waking up, getting a cup of coffee, kissing your spouse, go out and enjoy life with your spouse and kids, go for a weekly or perhaps monthly dinner with your family, and repeat these activities with commitment. It's also very easy for the relationship to become exhausted as a result of this. Each week, set aside one night for you and your spouse to spend time together, just the two of you. In the summer, go to a decent restaurant, watch a movie you both would like to see, and get ice cream. There is a plethora of options for a pleasant, romantic date night that both you and your partner deserve.

Share Daily Highs and Lows

Something along the lines of "for better or for worse" was undoubtedly written somewhere in your wedding vows. When it comes to your relationship, it's critical to express the "good and bad" daily. Make sharing a high point and a low point of each day an enjoyable dinnertime habit. This is something that the kids can participate in as well. Sharing one high and then one low with your partner each day is a great approach to keep your relationship strong.

Make it a Habit to Appreciate Your Spouse Each Day

This is a simple one as it is something that may be expressed or kept private. Daily, try to think of at least 1 thing you like about the spouse. Tell them, if possible. Tell your partner how much you love it if they bring you coffee in bed. Let your partner know how much you appreciate it when he takes the kids to gym class after work. There is no better type of motivation than having your spouse tell you how much they cherish the little things you do. And remembering the beautiful things your boyfriend does for you will undoubtedly come in handy when he is getting on the nerves a little more than average.

Tell the Partner Often the Reason for Loving Them

Butterflies and frequent verbal adoration characterize a relationship's early phases. As time passes, the trouble is that the butterflies and the "I love you because" statements fade away. It's natural not to be as "lovey-dovey" as you were when you first married, but don't abandon all verbal affection. Tell your sweetheart how much you love them regularly, but don't stop there. Let them know why you adore them. Whether it's for taking the kids to the market or when you need some downtime, or for simply being him and giving you flowers on a random evening, whatever it is, say it proudly and loudly.

Looking Each Other in the Eyes

Our parents taught us to look people in the eyes when we spoke to them as children. Eye contact is just as vital in relationships as it was when we were kids, so Mother and Father may have been onto something. When you are out with friends or chatting to your kids, having the person you're talking to

check their phone or glance around the room while you're talking maybe both disrespectful and annoying. It shows that the other person is uninterested in what you have to say or simply doesn't care. When you and the partner are conversing, the same rule applies. Words are less effective than actions. Instead of saying "I'm listening," show your partner that you're paying attention by staring him in the eyes and removing any other distractions while you're talking.

Spend Time Together

When it comes to making eye contact, turning off the television or computer now and then is a good idea to give the significant other your undivided attention, there's no disputing how troublesome technology could be, so make time for you and your partner to disconnect from it. Make a no-cell-phone rule for date night, as well as leave the electronics in the other room while you share a cup of coffee in the morning. Spending time with your spouse without the conspicuous distraction of technology helps give each other the careful consideration you both deserve.

Showing and Exhibiting Affection Towards Your Partner through Petty Acts

Marriage does not automatically imply that there will be no flirting. It only takes a simple brush of the hands or perhaps a kiss as you and your spouse walk past each other to keep the spark alive. A healthy relationship built on excellent communication and trust can genuinely benefit from a little romance and daily physical affection. Hold hands in public, hug the spouse from behind while they prepare breakfast, and give him or her a loving peck on the cheek while they read the newspaper. No matter how big or small the gesture; regular physical affection has a significant impact on a loving relationship.

Birthday Should Not Be the Only Surprise Day for the Partner

Who says surprises must be limited to holidays and birthdays? It's time to go beyond the yearly birthday cakes and Valentine's Day greeting cards. We are talking about unexpected twists and turns. You could even leave a love note on your partner car's seat one morning. A simple "I love you, have a wonderful day" with a few hearts strewn about might seem a little childish or silly. However, beautiful acts of kindness as well as romance worked well at the start of the relationship and will continue to do so in the future.

Do Not Mind Asking Open-Ended Questions

Talking about each other's days and what you had for lunch isn't the only way to communicate. It's about being willing to dig deep as well as learn everything you can about this person. Digging deep isn't always easy, particularly for those who have never felt comfortable talking about their emotions. It's also not necessary to have a heart-to-heart conversation with everyone. There are ways to accomplish this without forcing your partner to reveal their deepest secrets. Ask open-ended questions like "How was your day?" Did you have a good day?" Yes, they may respond with a one-word non-answer ("good," "fine," "the same"); however, asking open-ended questions allows them to share more if they wish. Keep in mind that not everyone is easy to open up to. If your partner isn't always sharing, be patient with them. We create emotional boundaries, and each person's limits are unique. As a result, be aware of and respectful of the emotional boundaries, just as they should be aware and respectful of yours. Finally, the more you learn about your partner on a deeper level, the more honest and open you will be with each other. And honesty engenders trust which are two crucial pillars of a successful relationship.

Try to Decode Nonverbal Cues

If your partner says, "My day was fine," but their tone is upset, irritated, or angry, there's a chance they're feeling something else they're not ready to express. It's not just about what we say, it's also about how we say it. More than just the words that come out of our mouths, our tone and attitude reveal a lot. It is, after all, a skill that is needed to detect nonverbal cues. Examine your significant other's facial expressions, hands (do they tremble or fidget?) and body language (do they make eye contact?). Do they have their arms crossed?). Also, pay attention to the tone of their voice.

Don't Try to Read the Mind of the Partner

You can sometimes tell how someone is feeling just by looking at them. It's not always easy and let us accept this fact. We aren't and shouldn't have to be mind readers, no matter how much we want to be. So, if you're unsure about how your partner feels, ask them. Take a moment to appreciate the fact that your partner is asking you what's up rather than ignoring the problem if you're the one holding things in and expecting the partner to read your mind. When you're ready to talk about it, do your best to let them know how you're feeling. It's not healthy to act as if you're fine when you're not, then blame the partner for not noticing. To the best of your ability, be honest about how you are feeling and try to express it positively before it blows up and someone says something they will regret. It is always preferable to be direct rather than passive aggressive. If your partner is passive-aggressive, tell them that it isn't good for either of you when they aren't honest about how they feel. Of course, it's fantastic when we understand each other so well that we can virtually read each other's minds and know exactly what to say at the correct times, but we're all human, and we may make mistakes or miss cues that our partner takes for granted. You both must work to understand one another better and be patient with one another.

Conversations Are Based on Reciprocity

Keep count of how many times you say "I," "You," or "We" as you converse with your partner. A conversation isn't really a conversation if it's all about you. Remember to return the conversation to the significant other and inquire about how they are feeling, what they are thinking, and what is going on in their lives. What is the context if you find yourself saying "You" a lot? Are you blaming and pointing fingers? Both people must have an equal say in how things are handled in a relationship. Both parties must feel heard and also be able to express themselves. It's important to let your partner know if you feel like they're dominating the conversation and you can't get a word in. They may be completely unaware that they are monopolizing the conversation. Conversations are similar to tennis matches in that they should flow naturally from one person to the next.

Schedule a Time for Daily Conversation

You must be excellent at communicating with one another openly and honestly. Since you have started sharing the same space, you've had to learn an entirely different way of being with each other. You should discuss the things that matter, (Such as how you spend your money) as well as the things that don't matter much. It is critical to talk about these issues because you will never know what matters to the other person unless you sit down with him to review it. We might well talk every day, but it's great to set aside time for something more meaningful with both of you so busy with work and life.

Tell the Partner What You Need from Them

Sometimes all you want to do is vent as well as feel validated by your partner, saying, "Yeah, that sucks, I'm sorry!" Other times, you require assistance. Because neither of the partners is a mind reader, it's critical to keep your partner up to date so that you're both on the same page. "I need to vent right now, and I'm not looking for any advice, just the support," or "I still need the advice on this situation," would let them know exactly what you need at the time. Being clear about what you require can also help to reduce miscommunication and stress in a situation. We can avoid unnecessary disagreements caused by miscommunication by informing your significant other ahead of time.

Should Have the Audacity to Say What You Must Say Each and Every Day

Now is the best time to put your world-class communication skills to work. Why wait to say what you need to say? You may never get the chance to say it. As well as it could be too late by the time you decide to express your feelings and thoughts. One of the worst communication skills is procrastination. It's so easy to get caught up in the minute details of life while putting off honest and accurate communication. Perhaps focusing on how much good it can do them could motivate us to ponder what we need to tell our loved ones while still having the chance.

Our loved ones require hearing from our hearts. We all have things we want to say, but we never seem to get around to it. At some other times, we wait for the right moment to arrive, but it never does. When we think about our family and romantic relationships, as well as our friends and coworkers, we must ask ourselves, "Why hasn't it been stated that we'd like to say?"

Cultivate a Healthy and Beneficial Communication Habit

It is strongly advised that you develop the habit of regularly digging deep and speaking from the heart with all of your loved ones. If there is anything else that needs to be said, now is the time to say it. Don't put it off. It'll probably be simpler than you think. It's more difficult not to say it. After all, it is an act of love to communicate with care, concern, and honesty. This is a difficult task for some people who have a difficult time speaking directly from their hearts. It is, however, possible to learn. The more you do it, the less complicated it becomes. All you have to do to start honing or improving your top communication skills is to remind yourself that no one in life will always be there. So, instead of leaving any cards on the table, why not attempt to get everything appropriate by the end of each day? Say what you have always wanted to say and say it now! Sure, you will have to find the right moment to bring up something vulnerable, but rather than putting it off indefinitely, you can do it now. For instance, if you believe your daughter is doing an excellent job as a new mother, tell her so and be specific. Pacify her. Show off your joy. She might be looking for your approval and praise. Tell her if you are sorry for ignoring her when she was younger. Also, spend some time discussing it with her. She, on the other contrary, will continue to struggle with it. Say it tonight if you've never given the spouse sufficient credit for the love and affection, they've shown you. And begin to alter your habits. Offer an apology to someone if you need to. Why put it off until tomorrow?

Do Not Be Scared of Talking about Anything that You Think Is Not Good for the Relationship

If you just get started, saying what you'd like to say is generally easier than you think. If you're afraid of something, do it anyway. You'll feel great about overcoming your fear. Best communication skills that work in any situation include transparency, honesty, and truthfulness. Consider how quickly time passes if you're reluctant to express what's on your mind.

13.2 Signs of a Healthy Relationship

Healthy relationships bring out the best inside you, as well as feel great about yourself. A healthy relationship does not have to be "perfect," and no one is healthy 100 percent of the time, but the behaviors listed below are ones you should attempt for in all of the relationships. Healthy relationships are characterized by open and honest communication; another important aspect of a healthy relationship is self-love. A healthy relationship has the following characteristics and behaviors.

Comfortable Pace

The relationship progresses at a pace that is pleasant for both parties. When you first meet someone, it's natural just to want to spend much time with them, but you must be both on the same page about how the relationship is progressing. You are not hurried or pressured in a healthy relationship to the point of feeling overwhelmed.

Trust

You have faith that your partner will not intentionally hurt you or end the relationship. Trust comes naturally in a healthy relationship, and you don't have to wonder about the other person's intentions and whether they have your back. They wouldn't ever put you through a "test" to prove your loyalty because they value your privacy.

Honesty

You can be honest and open without worrying about how the other person will react. You should never have to hide anything in a healthy relationship because you can tell each other the whole truth about life and feelings. They may disagree with what you have to say, but they will be considerate in their response to bad news.

Independence

Outside of the relationship, you have the freedom to be yourself. The other person should support your hobbies and relationships with other friends, family, and co-workers. The other person doesn't need to be aware of or involved in every aspect of your life. Being independent means being able to do what you want and allowing your partner to do the same.

Respect

You respect and admire each other's beliefs and opinions, and you love one another for who you are. You're confident in your ability to set boundaries and in the other person's willingness to follow them. They congratulate you on your accomplishments, encourage you to pursue your goals, and value your efforts.

Equality

The relationship appears to be balanced, and everyone contributes equally to its success. You don't let one person's preferences and opinions rule the conversation; instead, you listen to each other as well as make compromises when you disagree. You have the impression that your wants, needs, and interests are just as essential as the other person's. You may put in more (time, money, and emotional support) as compared to your partner at times, but the end result is always fair and balanced.

Kindness

You are compassionate and understanding toward one another, offering comfort and support. The other person in a healthy relationship would do things which they know would then make you happy. Kindness has to be a two-way street in your relationship, with both giving and receiving. You demonstrate empathy for the other person and their concerns.

Take Responsibility

You must take responsibility for your actions and words. You don't assign blame and are always willing to admit when you've made a mistake. When you make a mistake, you sincerely apologize and try to make positive changes to improve the relationship. Even if it wasn't your intention, you could take responsibility for the consequences of your words or actions had.

Healthy Conflict

Discussing issues openly and respectfully, as well as confronting disagreements without being judgmental. Any relationship will experience conflict at some point. It's natural for people to disagree, and that's perfectly fine. Recognizing the root issue and respectfully addressing it before it gets out of control into something bigger is the definition of healthy conflict. During an argument, nobody should belittle or yell.

Fun

You enjoy each other's company and bring out the best in each other. A happy and healthy relationship should be easy to maintain. You can have fun, laugh together, and be yourself because your relationship lifts your spirits rather than decreases them. No relationship is 100 percent enjoyable all of the time; however, the good times should far outnumber the bad.

13.3 The 3 Cs of a Happy Relationship

Relationships are built on stronger bonds and connections, but their foundations are built on three key virtues that are most prevalent in a relationship: communication, compromise, and commitment. Finding the right balance between all 3 can be difficult, but the most important thing is to find your way through it. Here's a rundown of the three C's that you should pay attention to in a relationship.

Communication

Half of your relationship's problems can be avoided or solved if you communicate effectively. Clearer communication can help you reconcile your differences and better understand your partner and the relationship. Non-verbal communication is just as important as verbal communication, as we all know. Working on your part will only help to strengthen your bond.

Compromise

The contributions of two people form a relationship, and it is the contribution of two people that strengthens the relationship and keeps the roots firmly entrenched. There will be times when you and your significant other do not agree on everything, and you will need to find a middle ground. Compromising doesn't always imply giving up your independence or freedom; it simply means that there are times when it's acceptable to take a backseat and then let the state of affairs take precedence over everything.

Commitment

Standing firm through thick as well as thin is more than a cliché. It has a deeper meaning in the lives of both partners. It means prioritizing each other as well as the relationship when it comes to navigating difficult times and emerging victorious, as well as giving each other the time and space to grow as individuals and as a couple, enriching and fulfilling your bond.

13.4 Relationship Tips and Suggestions

Given below are the top communication skills for cultivating strong and healthy relationships.

- People should not be used; instead, you must develop strong and healthy relationships with all who matter to you. Learn about them. You must not be reluctant to share yourself. But, most importantly, keep your attention on them rather than on yourself.
- Maintain your relationships. Try to keep them intact. Striving to keep the relationships up will help you form winning relationships that will stand the test of time. Don't forget or ignore someone. Keep them up to date with regard to your activities and plans.
- Be available to others. After the sale, don't forget about them. Please stay in touch. From time to time, send them your greetings. Speak with them. Now and then, send them a card. Make an extra effort,
- Congratulate them for their accomplishments and achievements
- Assign your relationships a high priority status as well as cultivate each one of them. Encourage and support the person. Take a keen interest in what others are up to. Enjoy having discussions with people on the contact list regularly. Pay attention. Inquire if there is anything

you could do to assist them in achieving their objectives. And then do it. Be sympathetic and kind. Happy relationships will enrich your life.

- Prioritize good, principled relationships.
- Take time to repair the rift if something goes wrong, including a misunderstanding or disagreement. It should be fixed.
- Now is the time to fix it. Do not defer it for long. It may be too late. Make a quick and decisive decision. You need to offer your sincere apologies for your role in the problem or incident. Relationships that are successful not only survive but thrive.
- You just need to communicate, talk and convey your concerns and apprehensions
- In every way, respect and honor the individual.
- Set professional boundaries and follow strict codes of ethics. Always adhere to ethical guidelines. Keep your boundaries in place. Always be completely dependable. Always follow the law.
- Maintain a positive attitude in your thoughts, words, and actions. Don't speak ill of or criticize others. Only use positive language. People will adore you because of it.
- Always be loyal to others and never stab them in the back.
- If you must end a relationship for any reason, do so in the best positive, sympathetic, and professional manner possible.
- Demand higher and higher standards of behavior from yourself; continue to grow and learn.
- In all your endeavors remain humble and open.
- Set a good example.
- When you want to tell someone how you feel, it's best to do so when the feeling is strong. Be consistent, and don't put it off.
- Not sure when it's appropriate to say something? Say it now: sometimes the best time is right now.
- Keep it simple and also be sincere as well as respectful in your communication.
- With a smile or a hug, and a positive tone of voice, say whatever good you have to say about the significant other
- Allow your words to have an extraordinary impact on your loved ones. Give sincere but creative compliments and praise that respects the person's life.
- If you remember that actions speak louder than words, don't fear using the word "love."

- Even bringing up a potentially contentious topic could be done in a supportive and compassionate manner. Consider the other person (the receiver) first and deliver your message helpfully and responsibly. You have quite a responsibility to both the receiver and yourself as the sender.
- Use simple language that the recipient will understand. Avoid being arrogant. The goal is to convey a message, not to demonstrate your oratorical prowess. Simplify the message and come up with new ways to keep it fresh as the conversation progresses.
- Avoid holding back and being as open, honest, and truthful as possible while remaining positive.
- It's sometimes better to concentrate on what someone (or the team) deserves to hear rather than what you want to say. For instance, you may wish to be critical, but doing so will almost certainly be counterproductive.

Bottom Line: Nurture your Bond Daily

Petty acts that manifest care and love should be performed every day to foster the bond between you. Such acts are essential for building healthy and positive relationships. Sending sweet text messages, kissing daily, unplugging during dinnertime, walking together, often touching, listening, asking the partner about their big meeting, their goals, happiness, and dreams; making eye contact; making love; sharing your feelings, and putting your partner first are a few examples of ways to strengthen your bond. It's also crucial to be able to recognize and pay attention to the impact your fears, as well as insecurities, have on the relationship. Remember that relationship satisfaction will ebb and flow, but if you practice returning to your 'why'—why am I in this relationship? Why is this relationship important to me? You would be able to solve the problems and build a healthy relationship.

Conclusion

Every interpersonal relationship is built on the foundation of communication. Effective communication is, in fact, the key to a happy and long-lasting relationship. Problems will inevitably arise if people do not communicate effectively with one another. Communication is critical in reducing misunderstandings and, as a result, strengthening interpersonal bonds. If individuals fail to express and reciprocate the feelings through various communication modes, a relationship begins to lose its charm. A healthy relationship requires a healthy interaction. It is often not necessary for a person to speak to express his or her feelings. Nonverbal modes of communication can also be used to express feelings. Your body language, gestures, facial expressions, and hand movements all convey information. Make sure you're not making any strange faces. For another person to cherish your presence, you should appear happy and contented. Don't always appear depressed and irritated. Eye movements play an important role in relationships as well. Your eyes alone can reveal whether you are unhappy, angry, or frustrated. You must also pay attention to your tone and pitch. Make sure you are not speaking too loudly or softly. It's possible that being too loud will cause harm to the other person. Speak softly and confidently. The other individual must be able to comprehend what you are trying to say. Furthermore, in relationships, word choice is crucial. Think about what you are going to say before you say it. Remember that a single incorrect word can completely alter the meaning of a conversation. The other person may misinterpret you, causing the relationship to fall apart. Try to be as concise as possible during conversation. Clearly express your emotions. Not attempt to perplex the other person. In relationships, being honest is beneficial. For a relationship to grow and

progress to the next level, a person must regularly interact with the other person. Speaking on the phone and sending text messages are two ways to communicate and stay in touch, especially in long-distance relationships where people rarely see each other. You must be courteous. Even if your partner has done something wrong, never yell at him. Talk about your concerns and try to work out the differences amicably. Abusing, fighting, and criticizing each other can sabotage a relationship and, in some cases, lead to its downfall. In a relationship, being disrespectful is a crime. Try to comprehend the other person's viewpoint as well. Listen with patience. You would never be able to effectively communicate unless you listen carefully. Email can also be used to communicate between people. If you don't have time to call the partner regularly, send him an email. The other person would be overjoyed, and feel being valued. In the workplace, emails are also a useful mode of communication. Try to communicate via written forms of communication for better workplace relations. Make sure the subject line and body of the email are self-explanatory. It is considered rude and loud to use capital letters in emails. You must not share any information with your coworkers verbally. Send him an email and keep your boss informed. All related employees must also be marked with a cc. If you discuss it orally, the other person may later refuse, causing you problems. If you want the relationships to grow and prosper, there is a golden rule to follow. Make your relationship your highest priority in life. The golden rule is to implement it. You are taking a chance when you do so. You prioritize the other person. You will find it much simple and easy to compromise as well as look for win-win solutions if you both make it a top priority. You go out of your way to help each other without being requested. All loving behaviors which improve your relationship stem from prioritizing that special person. We are insecure about our status at the beginning of a relationship, unsure of where we stand. We prioritize our relationships to achieve status certainty. Time moves on. We become at ease and secure. Everyone's relationship goes from being the most important to be one of many. Your personal goals and desires resurface. That isn't a problem at all. We need our space, but we forget about the tumultuous circumstances that forged our bond, as well as the risks and sacrifices we made to keep it safe and secure. We can become complacent as well as take things for granted. If you find yourself in this situation, set aside your other concerns as well as memorize the golden rule. There are many different kinds of relationships, all of which are vital to our health, happiness, and vitality. Relationships are easy to tinker with, never taking them seriously, but nothing is more important than relationships. Relationships are what keep the world moving. Relationships are more significant to one's happiness than anything else. You will have the keys to happiness and success and longevity if you master the relationships. As you make all kinds of relationships more cheerful and rewarding, your life will become more meaningful and richer. You will feel fulfilled and satisfied. For the rest of your life, you will be loved and cherished. Perhaps the happiest life is filled with meaningful relationships, meaningful work, and leisure time. You can master the relationships and gain a greater sense of fulfillment from them. It's never too late to start learning or improving your relationship and communication skills so you can begin to get more out of life.